She's Thinking Out Loud

by
Lisa C Hannon

LCHMedia

Texas

Praise for Lisa C Hannon and
She's Thinking Out Loud

"I was privileged to give Lisa her first managing editor's job, so that means I get credit for discovering her, right? Wrong. True talent doesn't need to be discovered; it reveals itself. I just had the good sense to stay out of the way. Read "She's Thinking Out Loud" and discover for yourself Lisa's talent for sharing insight, her caring heart and bringing about a smile or a tear. It's well worth the trip."

- *Hank Hargrave, Moser Community Media, former editor & publisher of The Madisonville Meteor.*

"Lisa's column has run in The Pioneer for years and continues to be one of our widest-read and most looked forward to columns. She has a knack for getting to the heart of a matter in a unique way. Her homespun approach to life situations always makes for an enjoyable read!"

- *Pam Palileo, publisher of The Fort Stockton Pioneer*

"Pertinent and deeply thoughtful quips from the heart. You'll want to read this over and over."

■ *Jody Bailey Day, author of Washout Express, Harbourlight Books/The Pelican Group.*

"Lisa C. Hannon is a rare find among writers. She has the unparalleled ability to match humor with reality. Her writing will always catch the reader in an emotional place. Whether it is joy, sadness, anger, or mirth, it will appeal to the reader's senses. Her style is addictive and appeals greatly to those who enjoy reading for pleasure and/or information. I highly recommend her works."

■ *Jamie Batson, author of I Survived the Attack of the Killer Boobie*

"Lisa Hannon has a way of capturing a moment, a thought, a memory and painting a vivid picture with her words. You will laugh. You will cry. You will be glad you read this book."

■ *Sarah Shuttleworth, author of Memories of Mint*

DEDICATION

Dedicated to Corey,
because he's everything;
and to Kelsey and John, Tyler and Haley,
because they're everything else.

With many thanks to Hank Hargrave,
the first person who believed in me enough
to put Managing Editor in front of my name.

And continuing gratitude to Pam Palileo,
Editor and Publisher of the Fort Stockton Pioneer,
who keeps Thinking Out Loud in print.

TABLE OF CONTENTS

Introduction

I started writing the newspaper column "Thinking Out Loud" in the <u>Madisonville Meteor</u> in Madisonville, Texas, in 1999. There are only a few pieces here from those first few years. The vast majority included in this book are from 2009-2010, when I began writing the column again in West Texas, and from late 2014 to mid-April 2015. This is when I began once more, and then stopped to gather them all up.

The reason there aren't that many from the early years is because most were basically hack jobs. Hey, just being up front.

I was a shiny new managing editor and I had a great mentor in Hank Hargrave, my publisher at the time, but everybody takes a little seasoning. I definitely took a grain of salt. Heck, I needed a whole bucket.

Fort Stockton, Texas, is the tiny town (population somewhere around 3,500) where the majority of these articles were first published in the weekly paper, <u>The Fort Stockton Pioneer</u>.

Publisher Pam Palileo is an extraordinarily tolerant woman, and seems happy to have someone local writing, no matter the subject… and as you can tell by the table of contents, the subjects have truly ranged far and wide.

She has provided, and continues to provide at this writing, a forum for a voice that can be anything from funny to serious to a little on the "running around behind the little animals" side.

I hope you enjoy reading them as much as I enjoyed writing them.

Please feel free to visit me at www.lisachannon.com, where you'll find all the other electronic places you can find me.

Make sure to use the middle initial if you search for me on the Internet, because my husband married two women with the same first name.

Not kidding.

It's why he calls me "Princess."

Showing there's a bright side to almost everything.

Lisa

May 2015

Why we write what we write

The question has been asked, "Why do you write what you write?" This may mean I'm clinically insane, because I asked it, and I'm also answering it. Hearing voices would mean I'm a nut job, but as long as both voices are mine, it's OK.

Right?

One of the big reasons I write happened recently when someone walked up to me, shook my hand, then hugged my neck and said "Thank you for this week's article!" and proceeded to explain why. That makes me feel like it's all worth it.

Luckily, I knew the person or it would have been a little weird.

I write, mostly, because when I don't write I'm just not right. And I don't mean "not right" as in "wrong," I mean "not right," as in following around behind the little animals making odd noises and flapping my arms. As in, "She just ain't right in the head, bless her heart."

But the second half of the question deserves a longer answer. I write what I write for a living. Right this minute, I write proposals for a high-tech staffing company. And, along with these pieces, I also write business articles on LinkedIn.com. I also write two blogs.

My first novel is selling in the tens so far. Not tens of anything, just tens. So far, the only writing that actually pays is the proposal writing — which is why I write those.

So, why write pieces for the paper?

Part of it is that I personally believe community newspapers like The Fort Stockton Pioneer will be the only ones that survive the Internet.

In the end, I think moving operations completely online will cut costs for big media to the point where they just can't resist the temptation. They can pay fewer people, and will no longer need printing presses. They'll be able to avoid ink costs, paper costs, junk their delivery fleets and fire their delivery people. All they have to do is put the news online and replace it with tomorrow's news.

Those big players may even be justified in believing the majority of their audience is connected to the Internet. And, eventually, news organizations will be willing to lose what they earn from the disconnected, as subscriptions just can't offset all the costs to create an ink-and-paper newspaper.

But, in this area where the haves have more and the have-nots so much less, the small-town newspapers like the Fort Stockton Pioneer, where these columns first see the light of day will continue to be a lifeline for finding jobs, for selling merchandise, selling houses, renting houses. They are even more important for life and death announcements, in ways that large city papers have already marginalized.

In small towns, people pick up the paper to see the pictures from their kid's play, and the neighbor's grown kid's engagement announcement, and their friend's Chamber of Commerce ribbon cutting for her new business. And then the coupons she has printed to entice new customers to check out her store.

The neighbor picks it up to see what's on sale today for groceries, and if her great-aunt's third cousin's obituary got to the newspaper office in time for this week's edition.

All these make me believe community newspapers will survive--and make me glad to be part of it. If even one person ponies up their extra quarters to buy a paper just to read my article, that makes me very happy (and the publisher, too, by the way).

To get back to the question, why do I write what I write? You have no idea how tempting it is to say I write because I'm an artist. Yes, writing is an art when it's done well. I have been brought to tears when reading a sentence that spoke to some part of my own experience.

We've all nodded in response to something we read, and laughed out loud when something flicks our sense of humor on the nose.

I honestly have to believe though, if I'm the one creating it, and I have to jump up and down and tell you it's art, well, it's probably not art.

So if it's not art, what is it?

I'm thinking out loud it's the handshake and hug I got because of one article. It's the message I got from a soldier in technical training, because his mama sent him one of my articles. That message is up on my wall, and I will keep it to remind me why I write any time I forget.

And I write because when I follow the little animals they get all cranky.

But mostly, I write the things I write because my daughter has, framed upon her wall, the article I wrote when she left for the military in 2009.

In the end, the right words matter.

She's Thinking Out Loud

Lisa C Hannon

Kids

A doctor told me when I was 25 years old that the surgery to enable me to get pregnant was unsuccessful. I was flat on my back on an X-ray table and tears were running into my ears as I sobbed. I knew it meant no children for me, ever.

I found out at 48, when I fell in love with Corey Hannon and then married him six months later, that I did not know jack.

We don't use the prefix "step" for anything, we never have. They may use "stepmother" to describe me to other people, but they've never used it in my hearing—and I love my kids, but "tactful" isn't a word I'd actually use to describe either one of them most of the time, so I'm thinking they don't think about it that way.

They're my kids and I'm their mom. When they're talking to me about their birth mother, they refer to her as "other mother." Works for me.

I wouldn't have missed this for the world.

"Stop choking me!"
"I'm not, I'm hugging you."

First and foremost, I want to apologize to any member of my family or extended family that I ever gave advice on child raising. For any sentence that started, "If I were you," and for every sentence that began, "If that child were mine, I would...," I am truly sorry.

I will do my best to never, ever do that again.

The explanation is mercifully short. I never had children of my own, and am now the proud parent of a boy and a girl, age 15 and 18, respectively, who came along as part of my soon-to-be-husband's life. And now mine.

And I am up the proverbial creek with nary a sign of a paddle.

I hope you can still hear me over the cackling laughter from my brothers and sisters, all nine of whom have raised children to adulthood. They believe this is my just desserts for years of peaceful living.

They may be right.

There are some things they could have warned me about, but noooo, they remained mum. Then again, none of us expected me to be starting over at this advanced age, nor could we have predicted that I'd fall in love with someone nine years younger than me, and with children.

Life has a funny way of reminding you that you aren't done yet.

So now, here I sit contemplating a 15-year-old who is nearly a foot taller than me, who would genuinely rather be at his friend's house. And, at his friend's house, he helps out with the chores, is polite, cheerful and pleasant, from all reports. Here at home, he would rather eat dirt than wash a dish.

The rule is he must come home on school nights. So, on those nights, he sits brooding at a table in the courtyard, or hangs out in his room, which we barely convinced him not to paint black, and watches movie after movie after movie.

When he's not here, which is more often than otherwise, I find myself worrying. Do all parents do this? I wonder if he's alive or dead, wonder how his father and I are going to survive the next two years, four months and two weeks until he reaches 18 (not that we're counting).

His father assures me that, when she was 15, the now-18-year-old was exactly the same, just being a girl, there was more um, verbalness and drama, shall we say.

I happened to arrive in her life after she had gotten through this particular place where parents are the stupidest people on the face of the planet.

What astounds me even more is the love that I feel for these two.

It's killing me that I will have less than a year with this person I now call my daughter. Four months from now, she'll enter the army, leaving the home her father and I have put together for her and her brother, and so impatient to be gone.

The new graduate has become such a part of my heart in such a short time. I've had even less time with my soon-to-be son, and as much of a mystery as I find his behavior, it is even more a mystery how I can love someone so much. Not just because he is so much like his father, but in his own right.

It amazes me daily that I can look at this person, no longer a boy, but nearly a man grown, who has a tendency to treat me like a convenience when I'm driving him somewhere and an inconvenience when I ask him to wash the dishes, and love him without reservation.

I know within reason the next few years are not going be easy, and I know I will grieve when he leaves home. I know these two are not mine by blood, but I hope they will someday realize how much I care, and how much they bring to my life merely by being here.

Ah, see, I knew I couldn't get through this without getting sappy. This parenting stuff is not for sissies, you know. I need to go find my stiff upper lip again. I know it's here somewhere; I always keep it close when I'm thinking out loud.

Teenager's time sense makes my brain want a nap

Time is, by its very nature, something of a slippery thing. It's not real, you know. It's a very human concept that probably rose out of the sense that we were moving forward.

Time is always relative to something else. "It's 20 minutes until 6 o'clock," means exactly the same as that moment expressed as 5:40, it's just that one uses 5 as the referent, as in 40 minutes past 5 o'clock, and one uses 6 as the referent. I know that's not exactly what Einstein meant by the theory of relativity, but I never understood that one, anyway.

My theory of relativity is in development, as I watch my 15-year-old son deal with time. Badly. Time seems to be the most frustrating piece of a world that frustrates him regularly. It is approximately forever in teenage time from now until he turns 16 years old.

It is also, apparently, forever if he has to wait for 20 minutes for a ride to his best friend's house. So, even though it's 102 degrees outside, and if he waited for 20 minutes he could get a ride in an air-conditioned vehicle, he's willing to walk.

On the other hand, when I ask him to do something, and express that I want him to do it "now," that's a little too fuzzy.

When I ask him the next day if it was done, the hurt look I'm given tries to convince me that I am nagging him without reason. The answer I get is "Oh, you mean NOW, now."

I swear, if I trusted the look in his eyes, I'd believe I'm getting stupider every day I'm around the boy. I will soon be drooling in my cornflakes.

I look at him, and the two and a half years we have until he turns 18 seem far, far too short. And it also seems like forever. Of course that may be the brain cells that I'm losing, apparently just from becoming his mother.

I'm thinking the simple fact of being a mother makes you able to hold two completely contradictory thoughts at the same time—like the urge to scream bloody murder existing right next to the urge to hug him and tell him it will be OK.

And that takes us straight back to the concept of time. I remember aching to be older. And oh my stars, how dramatic every single, solitary thing is when you're 15. Boys express it differently, sure, but the drama is still there.

He has to see his girlfriend or he's not going to make it. But she lives in another city, and neither one of them drive, and oh the pain of being apart. And time just leaps upon him and beats him about the head and shoulders.

It's time to take out the trash, time to get a move on, time to go to work, time to go to school, well, it's about time! And then, just when he thinks he's got things sorted out, he hears "Let's take some time and think about this," and it's time to take a break, and time heals all wounds, and it's time we did something about this, and timing is everything.

Lately, time seems to be a weapon that everyone is using against him. He knows he can't drive in Texas until he's 16 and not by himself until he's 18.

He spent a long time in another place where he pretty much took care of himself and now because he's in a happy, stable family, we really want to give him the chance to be 15 and not force him to grow up too fast, and that's really hard.

Because being in a happy, stable family means that a 15-year-old is not allowed to do everything he wants to, because we expect certain behaviors, and we are trying to give him time to grow up. But when you're 15, that is tyranny and oppression of the highest order, and depression and dark clothing and brooding silences follow, as night follows day.

Ah, well, when he smiles, it's like the sun breaking through an overcast sky, and I hold those moments to me, as they are precious and few.

I know when he says, "Mother...," the request that follows will savage my every instinct with that same horrible feeling that comes over me when the clock alarm wakes me from a dead sleep.

I think it's time to stop thinking out loud about time, before my brains explode. Think I need another cup of coffee. Wonder if I've got time?

Saying 'goodbye' to my daughter, 'hello' to my car keys

I began writing this on September 11, and I had to stop. I could not talk about my daughter going in the Army on the anniversary of those devastating acts of terrorism. Simply wasn't possible.

You may already know that, in the strictly legal sense, Kelsey Lorraine Hannon is my stepdaughter. Anything that starts with "step" and ends in any kind of relationship pushes a distance in between us that I refuse to tolerate. I married her father because I loved him beyond reason and couldn't imagine my life without him. With him came an added bonus, a son and a daughter.

When I met my daughter-to-be, she was 17 years old, cussed like a sailor, and was totally freaked out about whether she could pass the standardized Texas algebra test so she could finish school in December. Her father asked me if I'd tutor Kels.

Turned out it wasn't that she didn't understand the material, it was merely a lack of confidence in her own abilities. My tutoring consisted of teaching a few basic test-taking skills, and my faith that she knew the material.

She went in and passed it on the next try. And then came the best moment of all... when she got her scores a few weeks later, her dad was out in the field, and she came to my office fizzing over with joy because she had passed.

I hugged her neck, told her how proud I was of her, and heard my heart crack.

I've watched her change and mature across this year in ways that I would never have predicted. When she's upset, she used to whine at a level and in a tone that I swear only dogs could hear, "Whyyy...!" She doesn't do that anymore. She used to say "Ewwww!," every time she saw me kiss her dad. She doesn't do that anymore either, or at least not as much.

She taught me how and when to wear the color pink (however you want to, and any time you want to, that's how). She taught me you can be female and still be feisty and assertive along with it. She also taught me a child does not have to be born of your body to feel a mother's love.

I found out half my life ago I would never have my own, and thought I was over wanting to, really. But the first time I sat down with my husband-to-be to look at baby pictures of Kelsey and her brother, I burst into tears.

Believe me when I say I was way more shocked than anyone else. I think it was because my husband has those memories the snapshots represent, but I don't. Their birth mother has those memories, but I don't. I felt like an idiot for crying, but it wasn't possible to stop myself. Of course, then I had to try and explain why I was crying, and then I just felt like a big goober.

But, when Kelsey showed up in my office again just a few days later with tears in her eyes about leaving, my heart finished breaking. Whatever the world thinks, this is my child, my firstborn and only daughter, and I could only hug her and tell her she's doing the best thing.

Whatever my fears are for her future, they're my fears; I'm not going to burden her with them. The Army is truly the best way for her to assure herself of a future education and a career in healthcare. She's going in with a guaranteed bonus, and in a job that will keep her in a health-based field. And I'm hoping, in a field that will keep her safe.

That part of my mind that is gibbering at me that my baby girl is going to be in harm's way, well, I'm just trying to beat it into submission. Any time a child is further away than arm's length, they are in harm's way.

We have to let them go, right? I know there are instruction books out there for how to deal with this, but I haven't even had her for a year, there hasn't been time to read them!

In the past year I've gained a new husband, a daughter and a son.

I've watched my beautiful daughter finish school, graduate, fall in love, fall out of love, pack everything in her room three or four times, and get ready to depart my life in what seems like only moments since she entered it.

As I write this, she's only a little over an hour away from leaving. I do get my car keys back, but you know what? I'd rather have her still here running it out of gas on a weekly basis.

My life is on fast forward. I didn't get the chance to grow up along with her, but at least I've been given the chance to love my first and always-only daughter.

And I'm thinking out loud that I do.

It's gonna be an interesting year, dude!

Here's the deal. The rules the local schools are establishing this coming school year are not a uniform code. They're a dress code. Even on the school website, they are calling it "standardized clothing." And bluntly, no offense intended, but it's a dress code that is very well suited for working at Wal-Mart.

I am not saying this is a bad thing.

If you read my stuff at all, you'll know I spent four years in the military. A uniform code dictates what may be worn in terms of haircut length for men, hair accessories for women, jewelry, shoe and boot style, and so on, as well as what clothing must be worn.

This is not a uniform code.

I am wondering though, if it's been completely thought out.

The first time someone shows up at school in a shirt and pants that look as though they've been stuffed in a Pringle's can overnight, administrators will begin to understand that a dress code such as the one they've written simply doesn't cover everything.

They also haven't addressed anywhere what the "or else" is for not complying.

In other words, if my son doesn't wear the right belt to school, does he get sent home? If he wears his brand new corduroy pants with cuffs, does he get in-school suspension?

And no, we have not bought him corduroy pants, with or without cuffs. And if he wants a cardigan, he's going to have to get a job and buy one.

Why the sticking point? Because at my house, every time his dad hears the two words, "corduroy" and "cardigan," it triggers the same sentence: "Corduroys? Cardigans? Seriously? What year IS this, anyway?"

Personally, I think whoever proposed this dress code was a golfer who's tired of looking at rednecks out on the golf course in their cut-off blue jeans and "I'm With Stupid" tee-shirts.

This brings up some interesting questions, and it's possible they've already been answered elsewhere. Such as, what about the folks that can't afford to buy all new clothes for their kids?

It's going to take a year or so before these uniform items start showing up in the yard sales and the resale stores, so there aren't going to be any cheap uniform pieces to be found for a while.

Say you're a teacher and you've got a kid standing in front of you. You know her parents can't afford to buy her clothes, and she's in her big sister's hand-me-downs, and they don't comply with the new dress code.

What are you going to do? I know some of the public-minded organizations are contemplating assisting the kids that are in financial need, but don't know how that will turn out.

OK, now you have a child that has every piece of clothing directly in line with the dress code policy. She's got her capris corduroys on, uncuffed, and her properly colored cardigan. But she has on cat-vomit-colored socks, psychedelic shoestrings and glitter-soled shoes. She's within the letter of the law, but not the spirit. Your dress code doesn't address that.

Again, I'm not saying I'm against clothing standardization. Not at all.

Personally, I wish they'd addressed shoes, as well. The single most expensive item we buy for my son is shoes. At the moment, he's wearing steel-toed tennis shoes.

I asked him if he just felt like he needed to protect his feet, and if someone planned to attack them anytime soon.

He said, "Don't you remember when my friend, you know the one, the big one, chested my feet, like last summer, and I went 'Aahhhh!' And he went, 'Dude!'"

I kinda got stuck on trying to figure out what the heck "Chested my feet" means.

I'm thinking out loud it's gonna be an interesting year, dude!

If no one ever learns to lose, in the end we all lose

Been thinking a lot about benchmarks lately, and success. I've said before I'm not sure who decided that the one who dies with the most money is the winner. I'm pretty sure they're wrong, but the small fact I have zip for green stuff on a regular and ongoing basis probably prejudices that view somewhat.

However, I went and looked up the definition of "benchmark," and got lots of highly technical geological and business definitions. In my less high-toned vernacular, a benchmark is the place you mark as your own starting line.

So in thinking about all this, I have to say that giving trophies to every child who participates in an organized sport is a really good way to make that child believe he or she can win anything with zero effort.

The business about not keeping score in the games for younger kids is also not a good thing. It's not just annoying; it gives that child absolutely no reason to play again if the experience is the same every time.

And play for human beings, just like play in the rest of the animal kingdom, is the way we learn how our world works.

These well-meant efforts give our kids zero experience in how the real world actually operates. Nobody out here wins without effort. And nobody, but nobody, wins all the time.

What we're doing is raising an entire generation who don't know how to lose or win with any kind of grace. If all you do is win, and no one keeps score, then you never know where you are.

However, if you have a benchmark, you know exactly where you are, and you can figure out how to get from here to wherever it is you want to go.

I'm telling you right now, if losing makes you feels bad, and you don't want to do that again, you start learning how to win.

If you really do want to be that guy who dies with the most money, and you know you have none now, then the first thing you're going to do is go out and do some work and get some.

Here's the deal. At heart, we're all lazy. Most of us prefer to be napping on a Sunday afternoon rather than doing the chores.

You can take me as a good, ok, a bad example. I'm typing like mad in order to avoid finishing the laundry. This article proves that avoiding work is much harder, in the end, than working.

Trying to make a complex point in 700-800 words or less is not easy and pays bupkis.

The vast majority of us eventually learn that point, so we work because we must, in order to get money to do the things we want to do.

Participation awards pretty much ensure your child will be back living with you by the time they're 25. Because now you have a little girl who believes she should get a paycheck just for breathing. She won't last long in the work world.

And that little boy who believes he will get a scholarship when he's just coasting through high school making Cs to pass each year is going to get a rude awakening, too.

There are no scholarships that reward below-average grades, and there are dang few jobs that reward below-average performance, either.

There is one notable exception. Weather people can apparently be right about 12 percent of the time and still keep their jobs.

All that said, I do have filters that shape my viewpoint.

My husband and I are working toward a future together, one we believe we can create through setting goals and reaching them through hard work.

We've each lost a lot in our lives, made many mistakes and recovered again and again. Every triumph now is joyful, because we know how it feels to fail. And bluntly, we didn't like the feeling.

I'm thinking out loud that children need to know what losing feels like, or they will never know how it feels to win.

Because they won't.

And coming back to live with their parents when they're 25, or handing off their children to their parents to raise, is not winning.

Not by any stretch of the imagination.

How to go from zero to annoyed in 3.1 seconds— teenager not included

One of the many hazards of having a parent who writes opinion articles is that any disagreements may end up being worked out in front of the whole community (or at least the part of it that reads this page).

When I began this article, it was 10:30 a.m. on Saturday, and my almost-16-year-old son was hanging out in his room.

He had been awake for a little over an hour and I asked him to do two things. I still don't know whether he was actually that tired, or if it was just him avoiding the second chore, taking the trash out. The whole flap was a very successful test of my ability to go from zero to annoyed as all get-out in 3.1 seconds.

Yep, I am still able to do that.

Luckily for him and for me, the current sensitivity of my annoy-o-meter should be short-lived. By the time you read this, if the sellers get everything signed, and if closing goes off as scheduled, and if the electricity is turned on by then, my little family will be living in our new home.

I probably should clarify that, yes?

We're only moving four blocks.

Truly, in some ways it's easier to move cross-country. Moving a thousand miles makes you call a moving company almost immediately.

But everybody thinks they can move themselves when it's only four blocks.

Sigh. We are no exception.

This will be the fifth move in a year and a half for me. All but one of them have been upward moves in terms of accommodations, but five times is about four too many. I used up my entire weekend putting things in boxes and bags, and labeling things, and trying to remember how many closets were available, and so on.

Five transitions in 18 months is barely a patch on all the moving I've done since I turned 17 and left home. Overall, I've transferred all my belongings somewhere on the order of 30 times as an adult.

Granted, 20 of those moves were as an Air Force wife, and they hire folks to come get your stuff, but there is no easy way to move from one country to another.

This weekend, I spoke to old friends in California and Montana who made me feel quite a bit better about signing this mortgage. The friend in San Jose told me he is struggling to pay a $600,000 mortgage on a house now worth only $300,000.

It's not easy to muster up sympathy for someone whose house is worth more than a quarter million, but you can do it if you remember he still owes $550,000 for it. In other words, if he got a buyer right now, he would still owe a quarter million. Gack.

The friend in Montana told me it would be hard to buy a tarpaper shack in a flood zone there for less than $180,000.

Now, if you really want to, you can spend more than a quarter million on a house in this town. There's one in the listings right this minute.

In May of last year, it was dang near impossible to find a house to rent, and finding one to buy was even tougher. But by the time my husband and I decided to start looking, there were a number of houses for sale that were within our budget. And of course, once we move out of the condo, it will be going up for rent again, as well.

I know the reason so many places are available now is a direct result of the downturn in the economy, but in my vastly undereducated opinion on the subject, I don't think the West Texas housing market is in nearly as bad a shape as say, San Jose's.

I really am trying to keep from getting all het up about stuff, but seriously, the inside of my head looks a lot like the inside of my house.

If my house is all in an uproar, then so is my mind. I think maybe I'll go put something else in a box.

Oh, and the just-a-few-weeks-from-turning-16-years-old son did take out the trash in the end.

I'm thinking out loud that was a very good thing.

Got to 8-tracks, my car, even my kids late— I am a late adopter

There are people in this life who have to do everything first. They are the ones who bought the first car, they're the ones who bought the first laptop, they stand in line for movie premieres, all of that. I am not one of those people.

My name is Lisa, and I'm a late adopter.

What this does is allow me to buy the first generation of things cheap when the late adopters see the second generation on the horizon, mainly because the early adopters ditch the first gen stuff as soon as the second gen shows up. I also get good seats at the movie theater by waiting a couple weeks after the premiere.

Some of the things I purchased because I waited included a video cassette recorder with a remote on a 15-foot wire, and a microwave big enough to hide a body, as long as you cut it in small pieces. It was too heavy for me to lift.

I was late to adopt the answering machine, but couldn't avoid voicemail. But I now have a home phone without an answering machine or voicemail, very deliberately.

The reason? If I'm not there, I probably don't want to talk to you. Even if I am there, I may not want to talk to you. And I figure, if you really want to talk to me, you will call back when I'm there.

I also try very hard not to answer my other line on my cell phone or my office phone. It feels rude to say "This other person is more important than you are." I will call you back if I want to talk to you, I promise.

There are a few exceptions, like when they actually ARE more important than you are, but very few.

I got to eight-track tapes late, audio cassettes, video recording on video tapes, CDs, DVDs, DVRs, and I still do not want a refrigerator that tells me it's time to pick up milk.

Late adoption comes in handy when new technologies fail, as well. Does anyone remember Beta videocassettes? That's because they failed.

This may be why I live where I do. We are a tad behind the times in a number of areas, if you hadn't noticed. I really like it that way. In my opinion, the longer we wait on some of this stuff, the happier I will be.

The other one of the new-ish technologies that's scary for me is automated debit of bills from your bank account. I try not to ever agree to that. I don't want your picky fingers in my checking account, Mr. Car Salesman. And I don't have enough money to agree to that with a variable bill, like electricity or cell phones.

I also have a tendency to use things only partially. Like cell phones. Mine is pretty much just a phone with a clock, or at least it used to be. I didn't really start texting until I got kids of my own.

My son and my daughter have a tendency to text me bad news, rather than say things to my face. My son texted me a while back that he was ill and was going to stay home from school. He was in his room, and I was in the kitchen.

I'm thinking out loud this might be taking the technology thing a little too far.

Of course, I was late adopting him and his sister, too. Guess I didn't want to have kids until y'all had worked the kinks out of 'em.

But, you just have to lay down the rules and stand your ground. I told him he can't text me if he's sick any more, he has to call me to tell me he's not going to school.

That way, if my cell phone doesn't chirp at me by 7 a.m., I know he needs a ride.

Advice for my son—making marriage work

We found out right after Thanksgiving that our Air Force Senior Airman son, John, would be marrying his girlfriend, Valerie, the following Friday in Big Spring. We couldn't make it to the wedding, unfortunately.

But, I spent ten hours in a truck with my husband on Saturday driving down to Devine, Texas, and back. Gave me lots of time to think about all the things I didn't have the chance to say. So, here goes:

Talk about money. You need to know how the other one thinks about money, both in general, and specifically. Starting out, you need to set an amount you will talk to the other person about before you spend it. $50? $100? Considering how much enlisted airmen make in the U.S. Air Force, you might want to start at $20.

Don't try to fix everything for her. I'm not talking about putting light bulbs in and fixing door knobs that don't work. You should definitely fix those. Unless she's better at it, then let her do it.

When she comes home from work upset about something, the first words out of your mouth should not be your idea of what she can do to fix the issue. She just wants you to listen. If she wants you to help her fix it, she will ask. Any sentence from you which begins, "Well, you should…" is a mistake, unless she asks you directly, "What do you think I should do?" I cannot emphasize this enough.

Get separate bathrooms. Seriously, if you can't afford a second bathroom, make sure the lock works on the one you do have. No matter how close you are to each other, there are some things that should not be shared, and actions that should not be performed while in a small room with someone you love. Ever.

Cook for her. Or if you actually do cook all the time, then do something else she ordinarily does. Switch the laundry over without being asked. Make it plain you understand how much she does, and that you appreciate the things she does, by simply doing them every once in a while.

Be grateful for her. That's all. And let it show.

Be polite. Almost every couple I've seen that was headed for a breakup was no longer polite to each other. Being polite costs nothing, and means everything. Say "Please" when you ask her to do something, and say "Thank you" every time she does something. Say it every time she cooks, does the laundry, rubs your back, or does anything for you.

If she doesn't already say it, she will get the hint, I promise you, and start saying it back. It matters, when you've just finished the dishes, that someone says "Thank you, honey!"

Marriage is not 50/50. While each partner should certainly be putting all their effort into making it work, marriage is an ever-shifting, often lopsided equation. Sometimes it's 90-10 with the burden on you, and then sometimes it's 25-75 with the burden on her. It is almost never 50-50. Going to Devine, Texas, was not my choice. But I did want to spend Saturday with my husband, so I went.

Forget the word "divorce." If you don't ever bring it up as an option, then it never becomes an answer to a conflict. If you are unhappy, or she is unhappy, you will continue to work until you resolve the situation, as long as you don't believe that divorce is ever an answer.

Do things together. Play on a sports team, go out to movies, build furniture, go camping, go to the library, go shopping.

Do things apart. She's not an appendage, she's a human being, and some things you will do apart. I drive an hour away twice a month to go to a writers' group. It matters to me—and because it matters to me, it matters to my husband that I get that time for myself.

Remember that change is inevitable. You're both going to change. Gravity isn't anyone's friend. Time, children, circumstance, they change people. Love each other anyway.

There are so many other things—these are just the main ones that I can think of right now. There's one that's most important, though:

Laugh. The biggest, best thing you can do for each other is to make each other laugh. My husband, your father, makes me laugh every day. A lot. It makes my life an amazing place.

I make him laugh as well, although I'm thinking out loud that may be because I'm a complete goober.

Now I'll never have to worry again, right?

My daughter became engaged just last week to a soldier we first met over the Thanksgiving holiday.

While he was here, he got our blessing on his proposal. My daughter the soldier is a daddy's girl from the get-go, and he was intelligent enough to recognize that and ask her daddy for her hand in marriage. First point in his favor.

In the two weeks they were here, I also got to see him interact with our grandson, both in the happy and not-so-happy hours of any three-year-old with a mind of his own.

Second point in his favor. He understands that little boy, knows how to head off a melt-down, and still loves him without reservation.

Above all, he is patient with him. He did not try to be his friend, he made sure Tyler understood who was in charge, but they also had tremendous fun together. There is still enough of the youngster left in the man to really enjoy the time with little-boy toys, both old and new. Nobody in the world can fake it for that long.

I also happened to be in the vehicle when he got a speeding ticket. The young man's anger at being wrongfully accused was kept in check enough to keep the situation from escalating. It was not, by the way, a wrongful accusation; he was actually speeding, but nobody's perfect.

Everyone's stress levels go up sharply when you see that official vehicle do a quick u-turn behind you and the lights come on. I'll give him the point on this one pretty much the same way the officer gave him the warning. Slow your roll, buddy. Precious cargo on board. That's the third point.

Fourth point—he is much like his father-in-law to be. He thinks the world is funny, and he keeps my daughter from taking the world or herself too seriously. It's a gift—she has a type A personality that is often like mine was at her age, and he makes sure that the humor wins. That is not always easy.

He also knows when to let our daughter win—which wins him his fifth point. And won them a couple hundred pounds of elk meat to fill their freezer. Because she was the one who took the shot—and not every man of any age would be OK with handing over the rifle. If he wasn't, he never showed it.

There were a lot of other things in the way they interacted that told me they were good together—things that aren't that easy to put into words. You just know when two people are comfortable with each other, care for each other, want to be in each other's company.

Actions genuinely do speak louder than words, and their actions spoke volumes.

There are couples that just make me want to leave any room they enter. I may like or even love one of the pair when they are apart, but together, there is a dynamic that is... well, let's be charitable and call it uncomfortable. We did not meet Tyler's daddy until my daughter's relationship with him was already at that stage. And that is all I will ever have to say about her first marriage and my grandson's male progenitor in a public forum.

I wrote a piece on how to make a marriage work for my son just a short time ago, as he was getting married in December.

The ring on my daughter's finger means she, too, will be getting married. But it's her second, and she knows how to do it better this time, right? I think her father and I certainly did — but we were quite a bit older.

I do worry — my son told me once that it was part of the mom job description — but the only thing I can do is be here for them when it's time to talk.

Oh, and hopefully serve as a good example.

There are still a few things they can do. Like being totally upfront and honest about the baggage they've brought to the relationship, so they can chuck it all out the window together.

And not comparing this and any other relationship unless the current one is winning hands down.

So, I'm thinking out loud that my children are now both in loving relationships with good people. I don't have to worry about them anymore.

I can dust my hands off and say, "Done!"

Right?

Holding the granddaughter I never thought I'd see

Last week, for the first time in my life, I got to hold a human being in my arms who was less than an hour old. Most people have that experience before they are 25. I'm quite a bit more than 25.

I work with words; you may have noticed. But describing how I felt when I looked in Haley Leann Brewer's eyes, and she opened her eyes and looked at me, may well be the hardest thing I have ever tried to do.

It felt as if someone had punched me right in the chest. It was hard to get a deep breath, but nonetheless, I was grinning so wide it felt as if my lips were meeting in the back of my head.

I was almost scared to hold her, but I couldn't resist reaching out for her when her daddy held her out to me. She looked like a tiny pink burrito with a face peeking out.

I was able to cradle her tiny little fuzzy head in my hand, while the entire length of that so small body lay along my forearm. The rest of her amazing self, feet, legs, fingers, can only be described with variations of the word "tiny," so I'll spare you.

Things do work out like they're supposed to—I hadn't planned to leave for Missouri until March 21. The doctors planned to induce labor a week after that if Kelsey's water hadn't broken by then. The diagnosis of preeclampsia meant they were watching her very closely over the weeks prior.

Until I looked it up for this article, I hadn't realized that preeclampsia was once called "toxemia." I'm so glad I didn't learn that particular fact until now, as my ex-husband's mother lost her fifth child and died when he was nine years old, all due to toxemia. I would have been even more worried.

Even so, soon as I heard about the diagnosis, I decided to go up March 15. I arrived on Sunday afternoon and got the chance to have some quality time with the little family, my daughter, her husband Brian, and Tyler James. Tyler has been an only child for nearly four years, but was about to have his tiny little applecart upset in no uncertain terms.

The funny part to me was that I'm pretty sure Bella, the dog, knew before anyone else. Bella simply wouldn't leave my daughter alone Tuesday night. She wanted to be right beside her at all times, and was obviously upset.

Kelsey's regular appointment on Tuesday had shown a sudden weight gain of more than eight pounds in one week, plus high protein levels, and blood pressure they simply couldn't get back down to normal. All that pushed the docs into admitting her Wednesday morning.

An effort to mechanically induce labor Wednesday night left the two of us with images and sounds for me and painful memories for her that may never go away. After that was unsuccessful, she and husband Brian decided together that a C-section the next day was the best option.

I stayed the night with Tyler, as Brian was on a 24-hour shift at the hospital front desk. Did I mention they are both soldiers? No, I may have forgotten that. Since they both work in the hospital, Brian was able to check on her throughout the night.

To keep young Tyler on his regular schedule, Gramily (that would be me) got him up and going and off to daycare Thursday morning. We were both only mildly traumatized by the whole thing.

Sitting on the side of a bathtub, staring a little boy in the eyes and telling him he's not going to get off the potty until he's finished was one heck of a way to start the morning.

Luckily, his parental units had warned me that he would, indeed, try to pimp me over pre-child care, because he doesn't actually like to finish pooping in the morning. This leads, of course to later accidents. Things like this are when you question your very existence.

So, all the while he's saying, "But I'm froo, Gramily, I'm so froo," Gramily is saying "No, sir, you are not, you need to keep trying."

This is why young people have children. Old people no longer have the patience to do this every day.

So, we head off to drop the reluctant pooper at the child care, and then I only got lost three times on the way to the hospital. It's just the biggest building on the dang base, I don't know why I can't find it. Ah, there it is.

Then we wait.

Finally, they leave to have the surgery. I scoot back to the house for a quick shower, and find the house on the first try! Back to the hospital, and this time it's a record, I only get lost twice before finding the monstrous building.

I walk back in the room moments after Brian and the newest member of our family arrived. The docs kicked them out of the operating room to finish closing Kelsey's incision.

Holding that little baby burrito in my arms, I'm thinking out loud there was a reason why I left Texas when I did—and that it was worth every mile of the 1,800 that it took to hold my daughter's just-born, still sticky, slightly crusty child.

I'd do it all again in a heartbeat.

Aging

Aging's a funny thing, and you'll find these are actually the only pieces in this book where I've added dates. I'm figuring it might help you figure out where my head was at the time if you know what year it was when I wrote it.

Not scared of getting old, but not exactly checking out retirement homes, either.

Anybody wants to slap me in some old folk's home, they're going to have to catch me first.

Just saying.

The 100-watt light in my bathroom is hurting my self esteem

2000

I remember being a pre-teen—and what an awful term that is—and being told by a number of sources, including teachers, parents and books I was at that "awkward age." One assumes, with the current self-esteem savers in place, no one would use that term anymore.

I was at an awkward age then because I wasn't still a kid, or I didn't feel like I was anyway. I wasn't a teenager yet, and according to my father, teenagers were evil incarnate, so I wasn't looking forward to it too much, either.

When I did make it to teenager-hood, I was at yet another awkward age. Definitely wasn't a kid by then, and certainly wasn't a grown up. I could only get people to treat me like I was grown up when I didn't want them to, like when my father wanted me to get a job.

I got my first real paycheck at 14, but it still didn't make me an adult in the eyes of the world. I was out on my own at 17, which I did very badly to begin with. But, other than a short stint in basic training for the U.S. Air

Force, where I was a maggot and not quite human, I was finally an adult.

Twenty-one found me in Montana, respectably married, and terribly shocked when I found out someone else was an adult, but was younger than me. Still shocks me on occasion.

The next birthday is number 40, and it's headed for me like a semi-tractor-trailer rig rumbling toward a deer in the middle of the road.

I stand here, frozen, knowing it's going to run me over, and realize that, once more, I am at an awkward age. This one, though, is the one they don't tell you about.

For instance, I don't wear make-up—not out of any high-flown convictions, just too lazy to spend that much time and too cheap to spend that much money on my face. After all, I can't even see it most of the time.

But, because I don't wear makeup, those bathroom lights are absolutely merciless. I'm thinking about putting in a 40-watt bulb—that 100-watt sucker is depressing. I am a little bit vain, so while I don't use makeup, I do use lotions. Those, too, have their hazards. As I put wrinkle cream on my wrinkles and zit cream on my zits this morning, I found myself wondering, "If they meet somewhere in the middle, is my face going to explode?" That's one sign of an awkward age.

Financial planners want me to start thinking about retirement planning, but I'm still closer to my teenage years than I am to 65. Another sign.

Came across one of those dern lists of stuff kids today have never seen. Like record albums, eight-track tapes, skate keys and the like. I remember all of them. Heck, I had all of them. But, I've also been working with computers for more than 15 years, and feel like I'm part and parcel of the electronic wave of the future. That's probably another sign.

I use words like "dern," and "and the like," "heck," and "part and parcel." Yet one more sign. So is the fact that I'm not sure what "phat" means, but I'm pretty sure I'm phat.

I'm just thinking out loud I'm still at that awkward age.

When adults say "Your teen years are the best years of your life," they're lying

2009

I will turn the big five-zero next year, which I cling to believing is "middle-aged."

Of course, if you take the precise meaning of middle-aged, as in the center of your lifespan, that means I won't die until I'm a hundred years old, and I'm OK with that right now.

The worst part about being 49 is that nobody believes you. Somehow, the years ending in the number nine got to be the "That's my story and I'm sticking to it," years.

Personally, at a lot of different levels, I've loved getting older. Being young was kind of vaguely awful most of the time, and certainly confusing.

If anyone aged 13 to 18 actually reads this column, when an older person says, "These are the best years of your life," they're lying. The teen years are actually the worst years of your life by far. We saved the best for last.

But I guess I can't speak for men on this one; maybe the whole football hero/track star/big man on campus thing is more fun than it looks like from here. But for the women who remember their teen years with such nostalgia, think back one more time, OK?

I was on shaky ground during those years, but there was one thing I knew for certain in high school. I wanted to play basketball more than anything else. Anything. Unfortunately, I topped out at five foot one and three-quarter inches tall at 13 years old.

I played anyway. It was a guaranteed battering for your self-esteem when you were face-to-armpit with the girl trying to make a basket. I always knew who was shaving their pits and who wasn't, but not because I actually wanted to know.

Then again, nobody was asking me how my self-esteem was at that point. I'm pretty sure "self-esteem" came into the language sometime in the 1980s or '90s. Prior to that, we didn't have any and wouldn't have known what to do with it if we did.

So, my biggest ambition was to be a jock, but I was far too short and way too slow.

I was also too scared to be a bad girl, but it's not like there were that many opportunities anyway. Drugs didn't get to my high school until after I graduated — or maybe it was just that nobody offered me any.

It may have been that I was a little slow, too, thinking back. Every time someone asked me if

I wanted coke, I said yes, 'cause I loved Coca-Cola, and never got any soda at home.

Smoking and fighting in the parking lot was about as scandalous as it got.

There were four or five of us who hung out together, but I don't remember if we knew we were the brainy group.

We just knew we gravitated toward each other, and we knew we weren't the popular girls, the bad girls or the jocks. All of us stunk at sports, we didn't have the right name for the small town we grew up in, and we didn't even know what the "bad' in bad girl meant at the time. We were also an integrated group, which was unusual at the time. Now, we would be called a "diverse" group. We didn't think about it a whole lot, and nobody hassled us about it.

Was out of school a couple of months after 17, out of the house a couple months later, and turned 19 in Basic Training for the U.S. Air Force at Lackland Air Force Base in San Antonio. Turned out I was a little bit of a jock after all, or at least compared to the rest of my flight (the Air Force version of a platoon).

I won the mile run, and as the shortest person in the troop, ended up as a road guard, the poor sap standing there with their hand out stopping traffic so a flight could march by. I kind of liked it.

All that said, I never looked back at those teen years with any sense of, "I wish I could go back to being..." and pick any of those numbers. The only age that actually upset me was 25, because it meant I was in my late 20s. Turning 30 was kind of awesome, 40 was even better, so I expect 50 will be amazing.

Maybe it wasn't that way for you. Maybe you loved being a teenager. But, somebody had to be the popular boys and girls.

In my lifetime, I've seen the advent of personal computers, cell phones, Sleep Number beds, rollerblades, Walkmen, iPods, iPads, pet rocks and I Can't Believe It's Not Butter, among many other things.

What this tells me is that the Bible might have misspelled it. I think the geeks inherit the Earth.

I could be wrong.

Just thinking out loud, you know.

Not quite ready for a dirt nap yet

2010

I turn 50 next week. Yep, the big five-oh. Half a century. The age that, when I was 20, I was pretty sure was completely obsolete, ready-to-take-the-dirt-nap-but-too-stubborn-to-admit-it-old. Wrinkly.

I'll admit to wrinkly. In fact, I'm pretty sure I felt that last one pop up under my left eye this morning. Or perhaps I should say the most recent one. I'm pretty dang sure it won't actually be the last one.

And that, I think, is the hardest part about aging: we believe we must control the process. It's the reason why women spend a bajillion dollars a year on creams that will keep our faces from falling off the front of our heads. We struggle to maintain some control over our appearance. Men get distinguished. Women just get old, or at least we think we do.

I think, appearance aside, women actually do better than men at the whole getting older thing. I think men equate age with a loss of virility, and try hard to replace it with something else. At the same time, women are finding out that age means personal power—the ability to affect other people's lives as well as our own actually grows stronger as we age.

This is the time of their lives when men end up buying motorbikes, and women get their careers kicked into high gear.

Men buy Corvettes, women become CEOs.

Men turn in their current wrinkly wife for a fresh-faced replacement with a tight body and an IQ matching her shoe size.

Women—well, women are starting to do that too, minus the IQ thing. We tend to like smart younger men, and the fact they're good looking has nothing to do with it—and if you believe that, I have a bridge for sale across the Pecos River at a really good price.

I think, too, men become more restless as they turn this age—they carved out the path women are still struggling to get to in terms of successful career trajectories, and found success and satisfaction are two very different things.

Women, when they get to this age, have already found the satisfaction they were looking for in terms of home and family, and now begin to reach for success in their other personas.

I know that's probably sexist, I just don't care. In my opinion, women move their focus on their children and their husband's success to their own success as they get older.

A study in Minnesota from 2008 proves my point, not that I would be stupid enough to include statistics that don't. At the master's degree level, women 35 and over outnumbered men 61 percent to 39 percent in enrollment, and pretty much maintain that edge in terms of completion as well. So it seems fewer men than women are going back to get their master's and of those, fewer complete it than women.

And don't think that's because men already have their degrees — women outnumber men across the nation in enrollment at every level of education and at every age. But the difference is largest in those over 35.

So, to stagger back to the personal opinion side, I'm actually looking forward to turning 50, and the vast majority of the women I've spoken to agree with me as they get closer to this age.

In other words, when we're 20, we don't think we're going to like turning 50, but once we go through the 30s and 40s, 50 looks pretty good. Not least because we do begin to care less and less what other people think.

So, I would rather be 50 and a little foldy in places than be 20 again. Not that anyone's actually handing me the choice. But when you choose to enjoy what you have no choice but to endure, life gets a lot easier.

I'm thinking out loud it's kind of like deciding not to argue with the weather. Makes

the rain a little easier to deal with while you
wait for the rainbow to show up.

Unperforated, no writing on my butt, and living where I choose. I win!

2015

Why does it bother people if others know their age? I don't get it. It took a long time to get here, and I'd like to get a little credit for not walking out in front of a bus for all these years.

Now, of course, I live on a ranch—but I should still get credit for not walking out in front of one of the longhorns. Of course, they do move pretty slow. And, with a six-foot-something span of horns gently bobbling on necks that don't look they can hold up the weight, they're easy to spot.

I'm pretty sure I could outrun one of them on my good days, as long as I have a pretty good head start and an energy drink.

I remain unperforated, other than the times I've submitted voluntarily to surgery or other procedures where they stick holes in you in order to fix you. And tripping over the occasional cactus.

In terms of aging, I loved turning 50. I worry much less now what people think of me—

whether that means how I look, what I wear, what I do for a living, or anything else. OK, the fact that it took until I was 50 is kind of slow, I have to admit.

But women are, from birth, brainwashed into believing everyone is looking at us.

Please note there is one time that is actually true. Grandma actually is looking at you, and she doesn't want to see any writing on your backside. Or short-shorts. But it's not because she thinks you look bad in them—it's just she doesn't want creepy people looking at you. Or your backside. It's a grandma thing.

But regarding other people? The vast majority of non-creepy people aren't looking at you unless you're wearing a rainbow wig and flapping around like a chicken. Are you doing that?

Yeah, I'm not either. Today, anyway.

Turning 50 finally meant I was willing to accept I have a right to be powerful. That may sound a little odd—I'm not in a position of power. Not, at least, in the ways people often define power. No matter what their definition is, I define it as continuing to do what I love to do (like writing these pieces) and working from home.

These are choices. My choices that I made. For now, for today, that is my definition of powerful.

I can tell you from experience it was easy to lose sight of whether I could make my own choices, even as little as a year and a half ago.

I worked for a high-tech, billion-dollar firm, and was under so much stress I exploded more frequently than I care to admit.

Just to keep the record straight, when I say I "exploded," I mean I exploded verbally—I didn't actually explode, like bits of me all scattered across the room. I just yelled a lot, and sometimes I cried. And sometimes I did both.

I was scared to death to lose the salary I was making, because it was significant. My salary when I was laid off in October 2013 was more than my husband and I make together right now.

Not for the first time in my life, but I pray for the last, I understood at a very deep level what "money can't buy happiness" means. We had money, and I was unhappy every single day I was at work. It was killing me. In the literal sense—my immune system was so compromised that I ended up with pneumonia, just because my body could no longer handle the stress.

I survived until the inevitable layoff, and had the option to fight to re-enter that world. I also could have taken my experience to a competitor, one that could use my experience in the field.

Not to put too fine a point on it, I could have gotten paid boatloads of money. And probably been just as stressed out as I was before, but with a different business card.

Instead, after taking a year and a half off to lick my wounds and get back on my emotional feet, I chose a different company, on the periphery, not in the blast furnace.

And I also chose to work here, in the middle of umpty-thousand acres of land, with a husband whose job supplies us a place to live, while providing him with autonomy, trust in his abilities and reliance on his expertise and skills that makes him happy.

I'm thinking out loud you probably have choices too—more than you may be able to admit.

I'll be 55 in April. How old will you be? And how happy?

Remember, by not acting to change things, you're also choosing.

Change or die. Unintended consequences rock!

2015

I had reason recently to go looking for the definitions of "reinvention."

That search sent me reeling through a swampy soup of self-help drivel, intensely psychiatric discussions of clinical therapy, and quotations from a whole bunch of actors and actresses who were trying to spout something profound about their profession.

I was a little staggered by how common the idea is, and how far off the mark most of it was for what I was trying to express.

So, it must be time to write my own.

Take a breath, 'cause it sounds a little brutal at the beginning.

"If you don't change, you will die."

Look, you have to change, all of us must. It's kind of like the old aphorism from Heraclitus, who said. "You can't step into the same river twice."

We aren't the same people we were yesterday, but the changes from one day to the next are hard to see. The waters look the same in the river, but they're not. We may look the same, but we're not.

And then the day comes when the river floods from the spring snows, or when everything changes in your life, seemingly in an instant.

The day I signed up for the U.S. Air Force.

The day I began college at the ripe old age of 34.

The day I decided to have the gastric bypass surgery, and quit staggering toward a lingering death from diabetes, heart disease or a stroke, and began striding towards the hope of a long and happy life.

The day I met Corey Hannon.

I've lost a lot of things along the years, including my innocence, my illusions, and occasionally, my faith in humanity.

But I've gained so much every time I've reinvented myself—a career, an education, my life, faith in myself to make the right decisions, my amazing husband, two children who bring an incredible amount of joy to a life I thought would be forever childless, and now even two grandchildren (so far!).

It's the surprises that stick with you. I knew I loved their father, but I could never have imagined the love I feel for the 15- and 17-year-old people who were part of him then, and are part of both of us now, in their twenties. Huge, welcome, amazing surprises, constant ones.

I knew I'd lose weight from the gastric bypass. It came as a complete shock to find out I had gained the woman I should have been all along. When the weight left, she showed up.

Who knew I could be this person? I certainly didn't.

When I left my ex-husband, I regained my own family, in particular my relationship with my sister. It came as a surprise to me that we finally met and began to learn who we were as equals — not so much big sister, little sister, as just two women who have known each other all our lives, and who love each other deeply.

I would not have believed, more than a quarter of a century ago, after I was honorably discharged, that my time in the military would be important to me.

I would have been utterly wrong.

My daughter is a soldier in the U.S. Army, my son is an airman in the U.S. Air Force, and we are now a military family. My four-year enlistment in the Air Force that was over more than three decades ago means more to me now than it ever has. Surprise!

Every change I've gone through, big, small and in-between, began with a conscious decision to change the course of my personal river — but the unintended consequences have often far outweighed the original intent.

I may have no right, and I sure as heck don't have any certificates to counsel anyone on change. But if all you need for the job is experience, then just lie down on the couch.

I'm thinking out loud I can definitely tell you a story or two.

Lisa C Hannon

Money, the economy & work

Money affects all of us, sooner or later. Even those born with a silver spoon in their mouths have to pull that pacifier out to eat every now and then.

Money is a universal leveler, and I think it may be why we envy animals and children to a certain extent--because they just don't have to think about it.

Work, economy, money, none exist without the others. Which tail is wagging the dog today is pretty much the only question while you grab a cup of coffee and read one of these.

Money is what money does

Been thinking a lot lately about what exactly money is. Not about getting it, or having it, but what it actually is.

Money began as a symbol. You hand me your product, whatever you hunted or gathered or raised or grew, and I will hand you this bit of metal and you can use it to get other people's products.

Alternatively, you provide this service for me, such as a sword for hire, and again, in return, here's a bit of metal you can choose to use or save. Or, more likely, hand to the taxman.

It was never really as uncomplicated as a shiny bit of metal with Caesar's head embossed on it, though, not really. Money stirs every emotion we have.

People who were angry about money (as well as religion) founded the U.S. Remember "taxation without representation?" The colonists were ticked off that King George III was taking their hard-earned money, without a representative in the British Parliament that stood for the colony. The Boston Tea Party was a protest on this subject as well. We have a long history of getting bent out of shape about money.

But when you look at it, it's merely a piece of paper or a piece of metal. Both metal and paper money have their own peculiar smell. If paper money is old enough, that smell includes the original inks and paper components, now compounded with human sweat from bills crumpled and shoved into jean pockets, or held in leather wallets worn close to the body.

We have literally rubbed off on our money, and money has rubbed off on us. Every dime and dollar was earned with human sweat, as well.

We yearn for money if we don't have enough—and "enough" is a very slidy thing, changing from person to person, family to family, life to life.

If we have enough, we often give it away— to charities, to good causes, to churches. Sadly, some of us never feel we have enough to be able to give.

But we all know some who, even though they've never had enough in our estimation, never stop giving anyway.

Then there's the flip side—I knew an older couple who, through a combination of hard work and various inheritances, had well over a million dollars. It wasn't enough, though. They ached to have more. They struggled constantly with their financial advisor's suggestion that they must give some, and invest some in order to keep Uncle Sam from taxing them without mercy.

Their money hurt them daily, because they had to spend some of it to live, and they found letting loose of even that much quite hard.

They weren't holding onto the money to pass it on to people they loved. The money, in and of itself, became what was important to them, instead of what the money could accomplish.

He drove an ancient truck, and their house was falling down around them, in need of extensive repairs. They just didn't want to spend the money to get a new vehicle or fix their own house. There was never enough money in the world for them.

Guess what? They died anyway, and the money didn't go with them.

Every person who ever dreamed of winning the lottery trips over the conundrum that those most likely to play are those who can least afford it.

If you win the lottery, you are winning the contributions of those who are tendering their tiny stash of dollars in a bout of magical thinking.

They believed this would finally be the time they would hear their numbers called, and their life would be fixed, like nothing had ever been wrong with it. This time, they would get lucky, and have all the money they would ever need.

It's a piece of paper. It can be destroyed by water or by fire. It means nothing unless it's exchanged for something else — goods, services, shelter.

We seldom get through a day without using it or working to earn more of it. Every organization seeks it. Every person needs it in order to survive in this country. It is more of a moment-to-moment presence in our lives than we can even begin to realize. The drive to get more money has fueled every evil trade we have ever known, from slavery to prostitution.

Yet, it was also part of what made us rise up to become our own country.

A mixed blessing, money.

But, all in all, I'd still rather pull out my wallet than try to trade a chicken for a few loaves of bread.

Just thinking out loud.

For unparalleled in-home drama, ask your teenager to dust

We may yet look back on the early part of this century as The Great Depression: The Sequel. Unless they drag on for decades, depressions and recessions are usually diagnosed afterward, though, not while they are in progress.

Now is not the time to sit on our collective keister and wait for the next wave to hit, though. We need to start becoming active participants in our lives, instead of just letting things go on the way they are.

The following remedies may not work for you, but they're worth trying.

1) Don't put more than $10 in gas in your vehicle at any given time. My teen-aged daughter taught me this one. Until she started driving my car, I had honestly never even seen my low fuel indicator. Couldn't have even told you where it was on my dashboard. Now I'm getting very familiar with it. I tried filling the truck all the way up with gas, which left me in sticker shock. She drove it to school for three days. School is three miles away. When I got in it, the low

fuel light was on. Now, $10 is my limit. Don't care if gas goes back up to $4 a gallon. I'm sticking to it until she moves out.

2) Save on entertainment by asking the teenager to do something. Anything. Asked my 15-year-old son to dust the other night. What should have been a 20-minute, no-fuss job ended up being two hours of unparalleled drama, tragedy and the threat of murder and mayhem when his sister told him he missed a spot. This was narrowly averted by action from the parental units. Much cheaper than a movie and unlimited sequels as long as our patience holds out.

3) Encourage the teen-aged boy to stay at a friend's house. This one creates a number of economic benefits. You get a break on your food bill, 'cause the calories a 15-year-old, six-foot, 150-pound male can absorb are legendary. The friend's parents get a polite, well-mannered houseguest, as that's what your offspring morphs into the moment he enters their doorway. The friend gets help with the chores, as it's so much more fun to dust other people's crap than your own. The friend's parents' food bill goes up, but spending stimulates the economy, right? You're just encouraging that to happen.

4) Serve more leftovers. My ex-mother-in-law served food until it was gone. By Sunday night, there were 42 little bowls on

the table with a pea or two, three green beans, and various unidentifiable meat chunks that had dried to shoe leather consistency, each with its own glistening bit of fat permanently attached. My personal limit is three times served before I pitch it — and since the children don't like leftovers, it encourages #3 above, as long as I let them know ahead of time.

5) Encourage your children to get a job at a fast-food joint. Life lessons and free meals. It's like dinner and a show. Enough said.

6) If your children are too young to get a job: Put the little boogers out there with a lemonade stand. Cute sells, you know. Tell them they have to pay rent.

7) Better yet, send them to Grandma's for the summer. Tell Grandma you don't think they've bonded sufficiently, so they need to spend July and August there. This will make everyone happy but Grandma, who was going to take that singles cruise this summer. And the children might not like it either. But you'd be fine!

As I said, these tips aren't for everyone. All of y'all do not have children.

Six months ago, when I was single and living alone, I found I could make a $7.95 box of 18 corn dogs feed me for two weeks. Mostly because I'm not that fond of corn dogs. But, since I'm too lazy to actually do any more than microwave dinner, I would eat them anyway.

Corn dogs are kind of the perfect food. Corn is both a vegetable and a carbohydrate. The hot dog inside is made of three or four kinds of meat, so you get variety in your protein and fat. The stick could be fiber if you look at it just right. And, since it's on a stick, no silverware or plates to wash!

Disclaimer: You have to assume liability for taking any of these suggestions, because I'm just thinking out loud, you know.

If bagel choices symbolize universe divisions, what does that make cream cheese?

How many choices have you made today already? Coffee or tea? Drive down Main Street to go to work, or take all the side streets and wind your way around?

Maybe your decision was whether to yell at your son or daughter because they left damp towels on the bathroom floor yet again.

There's a theory out there that says every choice you make, significant or otherwise, begets a branching of the universe.

You decide to yell at your kid for being a slob, they take it as the last straw, run away, end up somewhere dangerous, and you lose them forever.

Or, at that same decision point, you choose not to yell, the kid picks up their clothes without you having to nag, and you begin a path to a stronger relationship with your child that means you get to meet your grandkids someday.

If the theory's correct, there are a kabillion worlds upon worlds out there. For instance, there's one where I chose not to go in the Air Force at 18, but instead married my redneck boyfriend, had six kids, never went to college, and now sit at my battered and scarred kitchen table bouncing a grandchild on my knee.

The little one just exceeded her diaper's absorbency rating, and I now have a wet spot on my leg.

In another, I never made the decision to do something about my weight, and am still living in Dallas in a loveless, childless, broken marriage. I weigh 450 pounds, have diabetes and heart disease, and only a few months left to live before I stroke out.

In another, I no longer exist at all, because my father did not change his mind as his finger began to tighten on the trigger of that .410 shotgun.

Whether or not you believe the theory, you must believe every choice you make leads to another and another.

Shaping your path is whether you believe there is a plan out there that shapes your choices — whether it's yours or a supreme beings — or you believe the world is completely random, there's no plan and it's all coincidence.

Got all that?

Here's what I know. It's not much.

I know my choices led me here.

At each of those intersections I chose to go left, right or straight on, and somehow ended up here, in a happy marriage, with two children, and a bright future stretching out in front of me.

Thinking each of my choices spawned another universe seems so full of pride, though. I find it awfully hard to believe the entire fate of this world, indeed of universes full of worlds depends on my choices.

Besides anything else, it's too confusing to think about. What's the choice level where this happens?

If I decide not to have a bagel this morning for breakfast, does that spawn a completely different universe?

Because I chose not to eat a bagel, that other world ends up being annihilated by nuclear war? Really?

If I truly believed that, I would become immobilized, afraid to make any choices.

I know some people who are like that. Frozen in place. Tired of their jobs, too scared to leave. Tired of their lives, too afraid to change that life.

I have to admit they're probably not immobilized because they're aware of the whole world-spawning theory.

Maybe it's just because they don't know what will happen next.

Guess what? None of us know what's going to happen next.

We make the best choices we can with the information we have available to us, and live with the results.

If you don't like where you are, whether physically or psychologically, you have a number of choices.

The first two that come to mind are a) try to fix it, or b) deal with it. Here's the kicker, though: Not choosing is still a choice.

Personally, I would rather make the active choice.

I absolutely, categorically refuse to sit still and let the world work on me.

It has led to some interesting results.

It hasn't always been easy, living with the choices I've made, but then, I have learned much, much more from my failures than I have from my successes. And, as Nietzsche said, "That which does not kill us makes us stronger."

I'm thinking out loud I'm not dead yet.

Positively thinking ourselves right off our economic tightrope

I just finished reading Barbara Ehrenreich's "Bright-Sided: How the Relentless Promotion of Positive Thinking has Undermined America." In spite of the grandiose title, it was a pretty good read.

Basically, her premise is that positive thinking at its worst becomes "blame the victim." Her prime example was her own bout with breast cancer. We are so embedded in the culture of remaining positive as a cancer patient that, if you do find yourself angry and raging about the injustice of ending up with cancer, you are told you're endangering your survival with your own anger. If you are to survive, you MUST be upbeat, you must smile.

There are a number of studies showing that people who remain positive and upbeat during a bout with cancer are more likely to survive longer.

There are also a number of other studies which show there is no discernible difference in survival length or rate that can be construed as a result of the patients' attitudes. I'll let you pick who you believe on that one.

However, I believe she's right that the sheer optimism that arose along with the positive thinking trend may very well be a large part of the economic downturn in the first decade of this millennium.

I believe rampant optimism allowed people to seek out adjustable rate mortgages with prohibitive payments when they adjusted. The optimism, of course, was in the belief they would get raises and promotions that would put those payments in reach. Or possibly the belief that tomorrow never comes... don't know which.

I also believe mortgage companies were irrationally optimistic to believe people would be able to pay those insanely high payments. In particular, they were optimistic to believe people who were already in credit trouble would be able to pay for more house than they could afford. That's what the subprime market was all about.

I also believe, however, if optimism hadn't been the genesis of the housing bubble which contributed greatly to the economic crisis when the bubble burst, it would have been something else.

Look at the patterns of the last hundred years in this country. Economies cycle endlessly and booms are inevitable, as are busts. Our best option is to balance on that tightrope and put away enough during the booms to deal with the busts.

The busts always come, and we're always surprised.

Thinking they won't come is just fooling yourself. Along those lines, one thing Ehrenreich touched on does get us into enormous trouble, and I've been just as guilty as anyone. It's sometimes called magical thinking.

Here's my two cents, and maybe even worth that much. If you are hoping and praying and believing you will win the big one, whatever that might happen to be, then you are human enough to notice only those occurrences which feed your belief.

OK, say you go every year to Las Vegas, and you've gone there for the last ten years. You believe you are going to strike it lucky the very next time you go, or you wouldn't keep going back and throwing money down that particular hole in the sand.

Because of that particular mindset, what you remember about previous trips to Vegas is how good it felt when you won, not the fact that, overall, you lost.

To bring it down to money, honey, you remember the $1,000 you won on a particular machine, but don't think too much about the trip to the blackjack table 20 minutes later where you lost that same $1,000 plus another $200.

Get where I'm going with this? We only keep the parts that feed the fantasy, not the parts that say it won't work.

That is exactly what happened with the economy. We kept holding on to the parts that fed the fantasy, like our house value went up last year, so it will just keep going up. We will get paid lots more next year than we're getting paid this year, so we can buy the bigger house.

And the bigger car.

And the swimming pool.

And the ginormous flat screen TV.

I'm thinking out loud the tightrope we walk between the booms and the busts is sometimes as wide as a superhighway, but just when you least expect it, it becomes a narrow wire once more.

The key is learning to walk it when it's tough, as well as when it's easy. I also think companies have to learn the exact same lesson on this one as people.

Use it up, wear it out, make it do, or do without

Did we go through a depression in 2008 and thereabouts?

I kept rewriting that sentence, but somehow, I just couldn't bring myself to put a capital "D" on that. "The Depression" was something I remember my parents talking about.

My most vivid memory was listening to them argue about who was poorer in the late 1920s and early 1930s. My father said quite proudly he remembered his mama sweeping the dirt floor in the cabin they lived in. My mother immediately won the contest, though, when she said the year she turned six, she could hear the horse whinnying all night long outside her window. He was mad 'cause they were living in his stall in the barn.

If you listened to the economic indicators on the radio and television and on the Internet, the only thing you could be certain of was you were going to get mixed messages. Even as I look at these numbers in 2015, I still don't know.

When they talk about "unemployment," is that the number of people who are unemployed? To my knowledge, they no longer count the people whose unemployment compensation has run out as being out of work. They just dropped them off the numbers of the unemployed.

So are we just reaching the limits of the first set of unemployment compensation given out, and people are starting to fall out of the system? Or are people actually getting jobs? I don't know, and I'm not sure if anyone else does either. The Bureau of Labor Statistics said at some point when things were at their worst that anyone who has not looked for work in the last four weeks is not unemployed; they just call them "discouraged workers." Good grief.

I'm thinking the next people that need to go on unemployment are the economists. I know it's kind of a "kill the messenger" sentiment, but I swear, the economists keep this stuff in unreadable language so they will continue to have jobs. Much like the persons who give the weather report, they still get to keep their jobs even if they only average being correct 12 percent of the time. Frustrating.

All of that said, I bless my lucky stars every day. Everyone in my family has jobs, including my 15-year-old son and 18-year-old daughter. My kids know how to go to work, and they know how to get a job and how to keep a job, and I couldn't be prouder of them.

OK, I would be prouder of my daughter if she knew how to get a dish from her bedroom into the kitchen before it grows green fur.

And I'd be prouder of my son if he hadn't spilled chocolate milk in his room. Smelled like something small died in there, and even after much vinegar and bleach action, still smells a little suspect. But they both do go to work, bless them.

Now I have to convince them that, even though they're working and they both have money, they cannot leave the outside door open when the air conditioner is running. I swear I was channeling my mother there for a few minutes, as I wanted to scream, "Are we trying to cool off all of West Texas?" However, I just gently said... "The electric bill doubled during July. Please close the door." I swear, if they keep doing it, I'm going to charge them rent to live with us.

Getting them to eat leftovers is not working, either. And they both turn up their nose at clothing bought at garage sales. If someone else wore it or used it, they don't want anything to do with it.

Don't tell them, OK, but every major piece of furniture in my house was either my husband's when we got married, or I bought it at a garage sale or a resale store.

Maybe it's a hangover from my mother, but I love shopping at garage sales. I bought my chest-of-drawers for $15, the buffet in my dining room for $20 at another sale. The blue leather couch I bought from the resale store. The loveseat I bought for $10 at a garage sale, and my sister spent $15 for material and tacks and reupholstered it for me. The two of us keep hearing our mother's voice: "Use it up, wear it out, make it do, or do without."

I'm just thinking out loud, but I'm thinking I might just try that one on my kids. I don't know, though, I really hate that raised eyebrow look that means I've said something untranslatable to the youth of the household. Really.

Think I'll charge them rent for that, too.

She's Thinking Out Loud

Humor

Sometimes, things are just funny.
Sometimes they're not.
I thought this stuff was funny.

Lisa C Hannon

There is a bigger difference between continent and incontinent than flammable and inflammable

I had someone tell me the other day they really like the stuff I write because they learn something from most of them.

I really appreciated the appreciation, but in thinking about what they said, I realized there are a few things I would like to learn, too.

For instance, I don't know why humans can't seem to get along. Because I'm lazy, I did only as much research as I had to on the Internet, but basically I couldn't find a single time in recorded history when someone wasn't fighting someone else.

World peace got pretty dang personal for me now that my kids are in the military. I don't want them in harm's way, and if that means the entire world needs to start getting along, I'm OK with that. It's time for everyone to shake hands and go to their separate corners.

Oh, and seriously, I've seen my daughter with PMS. And now she's carrying a gun. I'd duck if I were you.

Speaking of ducks, I don't know why we can't reconcile evolution and Christianity. Who else but a supreme being could design a system like evolution requiring umpty-thousand years to get from some little rat-dog looking thing to a horse? Personally, I'm having a hard time thinking past breakfast.

I also don't know why the U.S. is so schizophrenic about age. At 18 years old, you can legally buy cigarettes, drive, vote, and fight for your country but you can't drink alcohol. Huh?

And now I've said that, personally, I don't think anyone under 25 can make rational decisions. I certainly couldn't until I was 25. Probably 30. Maybe even later. Not that I'm saying we need to raise the drinking age to 30, don't get your knickers in a knot.

I also really don't know why drugs are illegal and alcohol is legal. Shouldn't it be a case of both or neither?

At first I thought it might be because alcohol had been around longer. I figure, as soon as some bright soul saw a raccoon drunk as Cooter Brown on fermented tree sap, we started trying to figure out how to get some of that for ourselves.

But when you look at history, drugs have actually been around at least 10 or 12 centuries and probably longer. We know there are recorded instances of opium trading in Mesopotamia.

Not that I think they ever called it Mesopotamia, and I had to look up where it was. The first thing I read showed it became Babylon, so I had to look that up, too.

Good grief, it turned out Babylon is actually Iraq. Those geography classes I took in high school a couple centuries ago obviously did not stick.

I also don't know why nobody I know has won the lottery. I'm pretty sure I've met at least four million people by now in this long and checkered life. Not one single one of them has won the lottery that I know of. They could have kept it a secret, though, I guess.

Huh. Maybe it's my turn, and that way all those people will have met someone that won the lottery. I'm willing to take that as an option.

I also don't know why computers didn't live up to their promise. I am old enough to have been working with computers for more than 25 years (yeek!). They were supposed to move us to the "paper-free" office. They didn't.

I don't know what the difference is between flammable and inflammable. I'm beginning to suspect there isn't one.

I mean, continent and incontinent mean totally different things.

Effect and affect are also confusing; I think we should pick one and get rid of the other one.

On that note, most people also seem to have a hard time with stationary and stationery, which drives me batty. Just as a reminder, if it's not moving, it has an "a," and if you can write a letter on it, it has an "e." So, stationery is stationary only when it is not moving. Better now?

I also don't know why most men think, when they've put the clothes in the washer, they have "done" the laundry. The laundry is not done until all the dirty clothes are clean, dry, folded or hung up, and put back where they go. Seriously.

Wow, that's only a partial list of the things I don't know.

I'm thinking out loud I'm just as ignorant as anybody else, I'm just more willing to admit it.

Please press "0" to speak to a human being. In India.

Here's the deal—and oh, my husband hates it when I start a sentence with "Here's the deal…"

I would not have called your business if I wanted to talk to a computer. I do not know the extension of the person I'm calling.

I do not want to press "2" for Spanish, and I do not want to press "6" to go back to the main menu.

I do not want to enter my Social Security number or my account number on a phone key pad.

I called you from a phone where I have to pull it away from my face to punch the numbers, because the keypad is on the phone itself.

Except it's a smartphone, and when I put it to my ear, it goes dark, and the keypad goes away, and then I have to figure out how to find it again, and I think I just put you on hold and missed half of the next message.

I do not want to hear another message. I want to speak to a human being who greets me with their company name, their own name, and the phrase, "How may I help you today?"

in a suitably perky voice. I would much rather listen to smarmy than go digital.

That would be because I particularly do not want to say my account number out loud, have it repeated back to me incorrectly, have to say "No," that it was incorrect, speak my account number out loud again, and finally descend verbally into whichever of the nether hells you are sending me to, apparently in direct retribution for every white lie I have ever told.

I swear I will never tell a lie again. If it will get me out of this horrendous process, next time, instead of saying "No, those pants look great," I will say what my niece says: "It's not the pants that make you look fat."

My husband has a lot more tolerance for this mess than I do. He actually likes answering the 800 number calls when they call the house. Yesterday, the phone rang, and a real human being asked for me: "Is Lisa Hannon there?" He said no, I was at work.

"Could you please give her our toll-free number, so she can return our call?" He said "Sure, but she won't call you." He knows me pretty well. He said the girl on the other end was pretty scandalized, though. "Well!" she says.

Even better was the call that came in last night. He says "Hello," and the computer-generated voice on the other end says, "Please stay on the line, we need to speak to you about..." whatever it was.

A few moments later another computer-generated voice says, "We're sorry, all customer representatives are busy, please hold." He didn't. He hung up. Scandalous.

Seriously, though, I just want to speak to a human being, and I genuinely prefer the first one I speak to can actually deal with my problem instead of putting me on hold and sending me off to another department.

Don't want on-hold elevator music, or to get caught singing "Do You Know the Way to San Jose?" by the person who eventually comes on the line.

There is supposedly a website address out there, http://gethuman.com/, that gives you the 800 numbers for a whole bunch of different companies, and the way to a human with the fewest numbers punched that are possible.

I'm thinking out loud, however, the person you get may be in India.

Here's another secret: If you keep repeating, "I cannot understand you, please get me someone who speaks English," they will eventually do so. Maybe.

You could press "0" to find out.

I'm sorry I said Mama's dachshund was taller than you and had more hair

I've been doing a lot of thinking lately about the nature of forgiveness. I know we need to give it, and I know I, for one find it much easier to give than to receive.

There are a few things, though, for which I believe I should ask forgiveness. Not always sure who's going to give it out, but I'll let you figure that one out for yourself.

I hope I am forgiven for thinking bad thoughts about my now-ex-mother-in-law when she told me I put the butter in the butter dish wrong. They were very, very bad thoughts.

I also ask forgiveness for being slightly glad my current husband's mother ran off some twenty-five years ago, and I would not have to deal with another mother-in-law. OK, I was really glad.

I devoutly hope I am forgiven for waiting until I was a whole lot older than I should have to get my pooky together. It's true women grow into themselves in different ways and at different times than men do, and I'm living proof.

I hope I can also be forgiven for the way I treated my little sister in our late teens and twenties. Oh my good gosh-a-mighty, I was such a snot and a snob, resisted every effort she made to save me, and said some awful things to her. Sorry, sis.

I think I've said this one before, but I'm also heartily sorry for every time I ever looked at the actions of a niece or nephew and told my brothers or sister, "If that was my kid, I would…," and finish the sentence any way you want.

Now I finally have a couple of kids of my own to finish raising, I realize I was an idiot to think I knew better than they did.

I am also very, very sorry, and hope I can be forgiven for every awful thing I did as a teenager. I am paying for them now, Mama.

Since you survived seven children's teenage years, I'm thinking I'm not paying near as much as you did, but I finally have the tiniest suspicion of what you went through.

To my much-loved niece whose balloon I popped without warning when you were about five years old, it's about time you forgave me, don't you think? I have bought you enough stuff now to make up for it and you're not allowed to blackmail me for more stuff. Capice?

Yes, I know I used a steak knife, but there were extenuating circumstances. Your uncle's buttheadedness at that very moment was beyond... oh, never mind, here's five bucks, I'm sorry.

Also, honey, I'm truly sorry your mama and I keep telling you you're really mine, and I just gave you to her to raise. It is fun to hear you say "nuh-UH!" but I'll try to refrain from that one from here on out, OK?

To the brother who is two years older than me, I will never tell a bald joke again if you'll quit with the fat jokes. I'll forgive you if you'll forgive me. Swear. Cross my heart.

To my other brother, I'm really, really sorry I said Mama's dachshund was taller than you and had more hair. In my defense, Mama started it.

To the state trooper who gave me a warning ticket the other day, I'm so sorry I forgot my turn signal, and incredibly grateful you only wrote me a warning. I would say I'll never do it again, but that would be a lie.

Is there such a thing as a forgiveness bank? I may need to make some withdrawals.

To my daughter, I'm sorry about the bad thoughts I had about you most likely losing the insurance card that was supposed to be in the truck that day. I probably forgot to put it in there, but I'll bet your ears were burning.

To my son, I hope I can be forgiven for really liking it a lot when you call me "Mom" accidentally, instead of "Mother." It's hard to be in this place for both of us, and I'm so glad you're here. The rest will work itself out.

To my brand-spanking-new husband, with whom I am much in love, I'm sorry it took so long to find you. It's not my fault you were up in Alaska all that time.

To those who read these articles and wonder what the heck is wrong with me, well, nothing that can't be cured, I'm hoping. But then, I'm just thinking out loud.

Life is a lesson plan with pigs, chickens and fruit

Do we have to learn something from everything that happens to us? It's a good question. The old saying goes, "Those who do not learn from history are doomed to repeat it." This is actually a misquote.

Santayana actually said, "Those who cannot remember the past are condemned to repeat it."

There's a difference between "learn" and "remember." I remember what I had for breakfast, but I didn't learn much from it.

Breakfast did bring to mind the old joke, though—what's the difference between being involved in something, and committed to something?

Well, in terms of breakfast, it's the difference between eggs and ham. The chicken is "involved." The pig, on the other hand, is "committed."

To get back to my original thought; for me, the misquotation regarding learning from history is actually the more apt of the two. It comes under the same heading as the old definition of insanity, which is doing the same thing over and over again and expecting different results.

If I keep doing what I've always done, I'll get what I've always gotten. Right? Right. So I quit doing that. Ended up married anyway.

I'm not really just thinking in quotations this morning, but they do tend to be snappy little bits of wisdom that can brighten up your day.

Most recent one I liked, though I don't know who said it originally: "Knowledge is when you know a tomato is a fruit. Wisdom is when you know you don't put tomatoes in fruit cocktail." Or something like that.

Not that I eat fruit cocktail. Or tomatoes. I don't like canned fruit, and tomatoes are just little pink wagon wheels filled with snot and seeds, as far as I'm concerned. I like tomato sauce, however.

The best part about being this age is the blessed ability to hold two completely conflicting thoughts in my head at the same time. I'm pretty sure absolute certainty is the province of the young. Not completely sure, just pretty sure.

Actually, I'm certain about very little except the fact I'm incredibly happy, vaguely sane, and apparently have zero sense of humor about my ownself.

At least according to my husband. He has a gift for making me really see myself. And he thinks I'm funny.

The first year of our lives together was quite an adjustment, and finding out he thinks I'm funny was one of the biggest ones. Somewhere on the road to becoming this great age, I had developed a teensy bit of overweening pride and a whole bunch of dignity. He puts up with neither one.

I have learned to turn quickly and look at him when he says something awful, and sure enough, the corner of his mouth does that thing that lets me know he is once more letting the air out of my ego balloon.

It was a year of learning many, many things for me. Some of them were from my marriage. Some of them were from my job. Some were from my relationships with family and friends.

Some were from having children of my own for the first time in my life. Some were intended lessons. Many were not. I learned more, I think, from the unanticipated lessons than from the intended ones.

And, much like the pig at breakfast time, I am committed. Not just to my marriage, but to all of it. To becoming whatever it is I'm supposed to become out of all of this. To doing it with style and panache and charm.

Or if I can't do it with those things, to at least go at it ninety-to-nothing, damn the torpedoes, full speed ahead.

I'm thinking out loud that what I learned from my history is I can't change the past...but I can surely change the future.

Chicken fingers and other fowl play

Maybe I don't think like everybody else. All I know is some things strike me as strange.

For instance, chicken fingers. Doesn't this bother anybody but me? The idea of chickens having fingers gives me the willies.

But then, I don't particularly like chickens. I like the taste of chicken. I just don't like chickens at what you might call the more… personal level.

I grew up with a chicken yard outside our back door, and it left me with a pretty low regard for the feathered fiends. They're noisy, not very bright, desperately need a good deodorant and they're hard to kill.

Once my brothers were old enough to leave home, the task of killing a chicken for dinner was left to my sister and me. Take two teenage girls, add in a dull hatchet and you've got a recipe for trouble.

I never actually injured my sister, but she'd probably claim some minor psychological damage from having to hold the little flappers while I hacked at them.

And speaking of my sister and chickens, she's the one my older brother convinced that new chickens could be grown from feathers.

Sis was maybe five years old, and she gathered up a dozen chicken feathers—we had plenty—and planted them in a couple of neat rows in the backyard.

She watered them and fussed over them for days. A couple weeks later, when they were all bedraggled and dirty and obviously non-productive, she went back to our older brother and told him they just weren't growing.

He told her she had planted old feathers, and they were like old seeds, they just weren't any good.

Mama wasn't too happy when she caught Sis pulling feathers out of one of the laying hens without benefit of anesthesia. The hen wasn't thrilled about it either.

Once I got grown and away from home, I figured out you can actually buy a naked chicken, all pre-de-feathered and wrapped in plastic. Somehow, it's never actually good plastic. It is going to leak on anything else you buy, no matter what.

I bought one. Took the plastic off, cooked it up whole, and it was awful.

It might have helped if I had taken the innards out. I also never watched her cook it, and knew nothing about spices, oil, any of that. I assumed you stuck it in a pan and stuck it in an oven until it was done.

I also knew there were guts in live chickens, because I was the one taking them out and taking the feathers off before handing it over to Mama for dinner. But, when the chicken is already naked and wrapped in plastic, I'm sure I can be excused for thinking it was also disemboweled.

It was polite of them to put them in a little bag, anyway.

Well, on the next one, I evicted the guts prior to cooking and took the chicken apart limb from limb to make sure nothing else was hiding in there.

My new-minted, Yankee husband (it was a long time ago) was pretty happy about the prospect of having Southern-fried chicken for dinner.

I had no flour in the house. But I did have Bisquick. Nobody ever mentioned Bisquick actually rises when you fry it.

By the time those chicken pieces were fully cooked, the drumsticks were as big around as my now-ex-husband's forearm, and just about as tasty. He ate the chicken anyway. Smart man. About that, anyway.

Since that time, I have preferred my chicken chopped and formed and unidentifiable. I do not want to know what the chicken used it for while she was still alive. Really.

I also do not want to know what chicken would do if they actually had fingers. Something rude, most likely.

No offense to all you chicken eaters and chicken farmers out there, you know. I'm just thinking out loud.

Worried about worrying about worrying

I happen to think I'm a pretty positive person, overall. My beloved husband, however, thinks I worry too much. He's started asking me what my "worry of the week" is now.

I've tried to explain that my best friend and I made a deal some years back. As long as we worry about stuff, it doesn't happen, so the reason the world continues to spin correctly on its axis (albeit a little wobbly, thus the whole season thing) is because we worry. A lot. But once we tell each other what we're worrying about, we have no problem dealing with it.

I do worry a little that I'm worrying too much, and I'd talk to her about it, but she's in Japan. So I have to talk to my husband about it, which makes him say I worry too much.

That said, worries do have a tendency to create such things as self-fulfilling prophecies — the mention of my ex-mother-in-law in another article is what got me to thinking about it. On reflection, I'm pretty sure the reason we didn't get along is because I worried about us not getting along.

I went into every visit with her pretty much expecting it was going to be really bad. And most of them turned out to be awful at some point or another. Which just fueled my expectation the next one would be horrendous as well.

Got to the point where I'd do almost anything to keep from going to see her. My avoiding her made her very unhappy, as well, thereby not improving the situation even a little bit. Pretty amazing how it just spirals out of control.

She wasn't a horrible human being. She was, however, a Yankee.

Now my current, and I am determined, last and final, husband tells me he's a southerner, because he's from Southern Alaska. But the lady in question was no Southerner. Although she did live in Southern Wisconsin. But I digress.

Yankees have a regrettable tendency toward a, shall we say, slightly more abrupt communication, bless their hearts.

The point—and I do have one here somewhere—is that a fairly large part of the problem with my ex-mother-in-law was my own fault. When we met, a year and a half after I married her middle son and the light of her life, she said, "Honey, I know you're not Catholic, what religion are you, exactly?"

To make a long, long story short, my father was allergic to religion, and my Mama was a Lutheran. The nearest church growing up was

Baptist on even Sundays, Methodist on odd Sundays, and if there was a fifth Sunday, it was a combined service, with dinner on the ground. My father insisted we not be baptized, but make the choice at the age of 12 what religion, if any, we were to follow. I made the choice to sleep in on Sundays. Because I was 12. The conversation in question was nine years later.

So my answer to my mother-in-law, because I was also a smart-alec of the first water, was "I'm a heathen."

It wasn't a good start. And me being me, I pretty much expected the rest of our interactions to turn out that way, and ta-da! I was right.

The original dysfunction was definitely hers — she made it plain I was not very high in her estimation, and like most people, I have a healthy ego. But in later years, she softened — even wanted me to call her "Mom." Kind of shook her up when I said "No, I have a perfectly good mother, thank you."

Now, that would have been the perfect time to heal that relationship, throw myself on her mercy, butter her up, call her "Mom."

I couldn't do it. The funny part about that was I never called my own mother "Mom." She was and always will be "Mama."

Years after I left my ex-husband, during one of our infrequent e-mail exchanges, he told me his mother was seriously ticked off because I hadn't sent her a Christmas card.

I fairly scorched his ears on the return, telling him you can only have a tug-of-war if people yank on the rope on both ends — and I had long since let go of the rope. One of the many blessed things that went along with divorcing that man was I no longer worry about my relationship with "The Voice of Doom."

Did I mention I called her that? Every time it was her voice on the other end of a ringing phone, someone was dead or dying.

Anyway, I'm thinking out loud there's a balance between worrying about something and preventing it from occurring and worrying about something and making it happen.

Next week's worry: The next oil spill in the Gulf of Mexico. I'm pretty sure I didn't make the last one happen. But not completely sure.

Being good at being stupid doesn't count

Newsflash! They lied. It turns out money DOES buy happiness. Well, it buys coffee, which at the moment is making me very dang happy.

I've come to find out as I've gotten older there are lots of things where "they" lied. Like for instance, "A barking dog never bites." My sister-in-law's evil Pomeranian doglet would still be barking at you while it had a piece of your calf in its sharp little teeth; it was a just a little muffled.

It may be I'm being deliberately obtuse today, you know, but I just feel like pointing a couple things out about a number of the old sayings out there:

"A penny saved is a penny earned." Shouldn't that be the other way around? Don't you have to earn one to save one?

"A watched pot never boils." Sure it does. At 212 degrees Fahrenheit at sea level, 100 degrees Centigrade. Your impatience is your own problem.

"An apple a day keeps the doctor away." My husband eats an apple each day and won't go to the doctor. Pretty sure that's not the original intent.

"Ask and it shall be given." Ever asked a banker for a loan when you were broke?

"Chickens will come home to roost." Actually, chickens are pretty dang stupid, and are just as likely to wander around until something kills them and eats them as they are to come home.

"Flattery will get you nowhere." This has usually been the opposite, in my experience.

"He who hesitates is lost." Unless, of course, he is hesitating at the edge of a cliff, which means he's smarter than he looks.

"Honesty is the best policy." Ever had a woman ask you, "Do these pants make me look fat?" Ever said "Yes."? Still think honesty is the best policy?

"It's not the heat, it's the humidity." When it's a hundred degrees outside, honey, it's the heat.

How many times have you heard, regarding the West Texas climate: "It's a dry heat." Well, so is an oven.

"Oil and water don't mix." They do if you shake them hard enough, long enough. Probably. At least they look like they're mixed, anyway.

"Opportunity never knocks twice." Opportunity beats a drumroll on your head almost every day; it's just a matter of what it's an opportunity for. Sometimes it's an opportunity to screw up.

"Time is money." Actually, I think it's kind of the other way around. What money buys you is time—time for leisure, time for travel, time to sit and do nothing. All of us are busy earning money in order to gain time.

"Two wrongs don't make a right." No, but three lefts do.

"When all you have are lemons, make lemonade." If all you have are lemons, you're going to be making lemon juice, not lemonade. You'll need to go borrow some sugar.

"You can't go home again." Sure you can. I go home every day.

I got tired of looking at the old sayings, and decided to go looking for some new ones. Here are a few memes I found around the Internet. The only criteria for making the list were they had to make me smile.

"I used to think I was indecisive, but now I'm not too sure."

"Death is life's way of telling you you're fired."

"If all else fails, throw up."

"Being good at being stupid doesn't count."

"They told me I was gullible... and I believed them."

"It's not an optical illusion, it just looks like one."

"Depression is just anger without enthusiasm."

"If you believe in telekinesis, raise my hand."

And, I'm thinking out loud I'm getting older, as well, so I had to end with a couple of sayings about aging:

"I don't remember being absent-minded."

"You know you're getting old when you don't do drugs anymore because you can get the same effect by just standing up too fast."

She's Thinking Out Loud

Lisa C Hannon

Bits and pieces

The only thing the title of this section actually proves is I'm allergic to the word "miscellaneous."

To stop abuse, you must leave, and to leave, you must believe you can

I understand how hard it is to wrench yourself out of the mindset that your world is unfixable.

As a child, when the person who is supposed to protect you and nurture you is the one who is hurting you, it causes disastrous confusion.

You can't blame your parent. You need and love them, so you blame yourself. You can't control whatever it is you're doing to make it happen, because that's not actually true. You're not making it happen. The pattern that both statements can't be true makes you freeze in place, and you just get hurt over and over again.

The style a child learns for explaining what is happening to them often continues through their adult life. We learn from our primary caregiver, usually our mother; then the other primary figures in our lives, teachers, the other parent, etc.; and then disastrous life events.

The style we absorb as a child is a big part of the reason why someone who's been abused becomes an abuser, or is drawn to someone who abuses them. Abusers are all about control, because they never had it, and the abused adult, usually a battered wife, but sometimes abused husbands, believe they have no control, and the world works on them.

The first relationship I had after I left home at 17 was me finding a carbon copy of my father and moving in with him. I went back to him three times after he beat the stuffing out of me, and he finally broke my nose when I left him in Albuquerque. It was the last time in this life I allowed myself to be physically abused. I broke that specific pattern.

I'm learning I didn't necessarily break the pattern of the mental abuse, however — I've had workplace bullies who treated me in similar fashion, and I reacted, in retrospect, just like an abused child. It's almost impossible to see while you're in the pattern.

Those who keep going back to their abuser are trapped in a pattern the docs called "learned helplessness." It's also known as "battered women's syndrome." For those watching from the outside, it is unbelievable and often devastating. "Why would they go back?"

From the side of the person being abused, it's perfectly understandable. They want to control you, and you want to be controlled, because that's what you've known all your life.

You may have had past non-abusive relationships, but they didn't last, because they simply didn't make sense to you. They make you completely paranoid, because you find yourself ducking, dodging, waiting for them to get mad at you. Wondering what it will take to push their buttons enough to hit you.

And in the end, you don't respect them because they don't hit you, and you have no idea how to explain that to anyone. You don't actually want them to hit you. "Love" to you just means something different than it does to someone who's never been abused.

But now, there is a child in the picture. Your child, or children.

You're getting abused. And you can't blame your partner, because you need and love them, so you blame yourself, but you can't control whatever it is you're doing to make it happen, because that's not actually true. Again.

So you become immobilized, and you get hurt. Over and over again. As do your children. And if you think it doesn't affect your children because you're the only one who's getting hit, you're wrong.

Forty years later, I can still hear my father's hand hitting my mother's face.

You don't deserve the pain. No one does. And if you are getting hit, your child is next. Abuse doesn't stop. And no matter how many times he (or she) tells you they're sorry and they'll never do it again, it's a lie.

It doesn't stop. I promise you—from someone who was there, as a child and as a woman.

While you are still living in the house with the person who is hitting you: It. Does. Not. Stop.

I'm thinking out loud, as loud as I can, and if I knew how to shout in print, I would. To stop the pain, get out. And the first step to getting out is to believe you control your life.

You must believe you don't deserve the pain. And if you can't believe that, then you need to believe that your children don't.

Refinishing furniture just makes the world a better place

I love garage sales, and whenever we live near each other, my sis and I go every Saturday morning. Thank goodness the weather is beginning to cooperate, so there are more than just a few. I swear I see some of the same stuff I saw last year showing up at someone else's garage sale this spring. Or maybe it's just all starting to run together.

Furniture, wood furniture specifically, is one of my greatest weaknesses. A bookshelf or an armoire will make me hit my brakes faster than anything else when we're out looking for the next great buy.

Recently bought an in-wall ironing board, built into a cabinet, which may or may not be an antique. Didn't buy the wall, just the ironing board and cabinet.

It's just one of those weird things I've always wanted when I saw them in someone else's house. It wasn't like go-out-and-buy-one-right-now wanted, more like the-next-time-I-see-one-of-those-at-a-garage-sale-I'm-buying-it wanted. So I did. My husband pointed out that I don't iron. I pointed out that the big white box in the laundry room where the clothes go round and round and get nice and warm and pull all the wrinkles out serves the same purpose with almost no effort.

Anyway, about two weeks after I brought it home, after I had moved it around the carport two or three times, my most-beloved husband tackled creating the hole in the wall to put it in. Which meant I had to get it refinished. Like right then.

I am, apparently, an incurable optimist. I am also, apparently, clinically insane to believe I could get every speck of paint off the inset panels gracing the outside of the cabinet door.

In order to begin getting the old paint off, you have to wear gloves heavy enough to keep the refinishing gel chemicals from seeping through.

Here's a hint. Never, ever, answer your 16-year-old's question, "What are you going to Wal-Mart for?" with the short phrase, "Stripper gloves." Makes them give you a really funny look.

Whoever painted this thing the first time, bless their hearts, did not seal the wood in any way. Paint sinks into unsealed wood grain. Deeply. I got so frustrated with trying to get paint off the dang thing, I called my sister to bring over her orbital sander, which helped a lot.

With the heavy-duty sandpaper on that thing, it will take the finish off a piece of furniture quicker than you can spit. Sure enough, it was the only thing that would get the paint off of those inset panels. Unfortunately, its round, so it won't get in the corners. Thus the ouchy thumb, from sanding corners and edges. Pretty sure I have no fingerprints now, either.

After using a couple of different electric tools to finish this piece, I started getting very philosophical about the whole thing.

Power may not corrupt, but it can certainly leave scars. Those scars remain on both the user and on the entity being altered through the use of power.

I can also tell you that the use of power doesn't take care of everything; there are some things that need finesse. I'm beginning to learn finesse, but it's taken me about 50 years.

I have learned over the years, though, time's damages can be turned into assets if you look at it right — and I'm not sure the 40-year-old me would have noticed that one.

I'm thinking out loud I can also tell you why I refinish furniture — because bring something that was scarred and stained and scratched back to become something beautiful again satisfies something deep inside my soul.

I think if I was evil, my mama would have told me

The initial publication of these pieces is in a small town, weekly newspaper, and I get some interesting responses to them; taken as a whole most of them are positive.

There is, however, one kind of response that baffles me. More than one person has told me they think I'm very brave to talk about my past, present and future in this public forum.

Now, I'm an awful lot of things, but I'm not sure "brave" is the adjective I would choose. I do understand, and really appreciate the sentiment, but this isn't bravery, this is fatigue.

I live my life as wide open as humanly possible, not because I think that's anything special, but because I am tired of secrets.

Don't get me wrong, there is a big difference between secrecy and confidentiality. Confidentiality is necessary in a number of different arenas, especially where people's finances, health, and other information that could possibly cause them pain are concerned. Confidentiality is a necessity in the world we live in. I'm not talking about that.

I'm talking about the personal secrets that impact lives beside your own. I'm talking about the ones like my now-ex-husband's secret that my now-ex-mother-in-law shared with me as I was crossing the Red River into Texas, leaving her son behind in Illinois for good.

His secret to tell, not mine, but because it was out there, and held close for 27 years, his entire masquerade of "I always tell the truth; don't ask the question if you don't want to hear the answer," shattered, like a cold glass filled with boiling water. His entire persona failed under scrutiny. Our whole lives together ended up as one big lie.

And that is what I object to most about secrets. Big, honking secrets inevitably seem to generate lies.

For instance, A knows B secretly hates C, which causes A to lie to C, so they don't hurt C or rat out B. It also means B lies every time they speak cordially to C, because what they really want to do is throw a rock at 'em.

Please take note I am not telling you it's OK to go around throwing rocks at people just because you hate them. Don't do that.

But, as Snoopy would say, bleah, or pthbbbbthpf. Trying to make a sound of disgust in print isn't easy, but I'm telling you right now, I'm done.

So don't tell me, especially if you want it to be a secret. And, if it's truly a secret, why are you telling people, anyway? If you have said it to even one person already, I'll give you a hint, it's probably not a secret. Especially in a small town.

I'm sure you've heard it said everybody knows your business in a small town. That's a fact. I grew up in a small town. And if they don't know what you're doing, they will make something up.

There have been a fair few unfounded rumors about me, and I usually find out about them when people say something interesting like, "You're not at all like so-and-so said you were!"

Some of these rumors include that I'm gay, and I'm thinking my brand-new husband would be a little upset about that, but my favorite is the rumor that's making the rounds that I'm evil.

Well, I guess it's a rumor, but then again, maybe it's an opinion. But I guess evil is in the eye of the beholder, as well as beauty.

I don't personally think I'm evil, but then, who does believe that of themselves? If I were evil, would I know?

Just to make it clear, I'm not gay, and I think if were evil, my mama would have told me.

And that's how secrets devolve into rumors and lies. I have moved from being very brave and at the beginning of this article to being straight and Miss Goody Two-Shoes by the end of it.

It's like that children's game where you start a rumor on one side of the room, and by the time it gets all the way around, it's something different.

Bad secrets change, grow, and morph into the biggest thing in the room, and they spawn lies, creating them from nothing, bringing them into being with lives of their own.

And that is exactly what secrets do. Unless it's a good secret, like you're about to do something really nice for someone else, just don't tell me.

I'm thinking out loud I'm just going to go take a nap. Secrets make me tired.

Gastric surgery isn't a magic bullet for your life

My health-care professional asked me to write this, because a) she's an amazing person, and b) she's seeing more and more people come through who are finding cheap gastric surgeries more readily available in the next country over. I usually try to write to a broad audience, but this is for those who are contemplating weight-loss surgery.

If you know me, you know I had a gastric bypass ten years ago. I don't hide it. It was necessary to save my life at the time. I was categorized as "super-obese," I was pre-diabetic and I had tried every diet known to man. After 30 years of dieting, I weighed more than 300 pounds at 5'2" tall. I was literally bigger around than I was tall—and it wasn't getting better, it was getting worse.

After a lot of psychological counseling, I had surgery in September 2005.

The first three years of losing weight pretty much shot my marriage in the head—which is just one of the things you're risking.

I found my confidence and I found my smile. I worked in a couple of image-based jobs, including fitness director and flight attendant. All told, I dropped a total of 166 pounds off my now tiny frame, and I was able to walk without pain for the first time in more than a decade. I dropped from a size 36W to a size six jeans, from a size XXXL in shirts to a small.

Once I shed the baggage of my old life, I came to stay with family in Texas, and here I found the love of my life, who came with a 15- and a 17-year-old who called me "Mom" from the jump. Four years after my surgery, I married him here in Fort Stockton. June will be our sixth anniversary. Our teens are now in the military and married. We're grandparents, and if I get any happier, I'm going to have to sit on my hands to stop me waving at people.

Sounds like magic, right?

Two and a half years ago, I landed in an emergency room in Oregon, doubled over, screaming, because my original surgeon had left a tiny hole, which my entire intestine migrated through and then twisted.

I was a few hours from death, but chanced onto an emergency surgeon willing to ignore the CT scan's lack of evidence and open me up. That was six weeks of recovery time.

The restriction of the original gastric bypass surgery still works. I can still eat only about a cup of solid food at a time. The key word is "solid."

Unfortunately, high-calorie, crunchy, salty chips, crackers and popcorn slide through the restrictions quite easily.

Like a small percentage of those who have the surgery, I ended up with something called "dumping syndrome." If I eat a varying amount of sugar, I get pale, sweaty, shaky, ill and then there are more unpleasant consequences. This can happen anywhere from 15 minutes to two hours after ingesting the sugar.

So, last week, I ate some gummy candies that pushed me into one of these episodes. My husband's sympathy level was pretty much non-existent. His only comment was, "The woman I married wouldn't even look at that much sugar."

And he's right. So why did I pick them up? Because they didn't operate on my head, they operated on my stomach. And there's still a 300-pound woman's addiction that drives me past reason.

Eating like that, I've gained enough weight that I can feel the way I walk starting to change. My knees hurt so much I'm on prescription medications, and have been for the last three years. Every single pound I put back on adds another four pounds to the jolt my joints suffer.

I've regained 42 percent of the 166 pounds I lost. I'll let you do the math.

So, I'm back with my health professional, on a medically-supervised diet, with regular counseling with her, because this journey isn't over. Surgery just wasn't a magic bullet.

I'm trying to help you understand, you're still going to have a fat person's appetite and drive to eat inside you. You will never fill that empty place, because it was never really your stomach.

I tried to put a stake through my 300-pound woman's heart ten years ago—but she's surprisingly agile for a fat girl. Her appetites and need for food to fill her empty spaces will never go away, and I'm still trying to find a way to live with her.

Now, have the last 10 years been worth it? Yes, a thousand times yes.

Have the last 10 years been easy?

I'm thinking out loud, if you read this and believe it's been easy, I didn't write it right.

Just...think. Think really hard.

My toothbrush might be a ratfink, but my refrigerator keeps my secrets

If you're hanging around on the bleeding edge of technology these days--most of us aren't--you may be aware of a concept that's been barreling down upon us for some time now called the "Internet of Things."

Wikipedia defines it as "the interconnection of uniquely identifiable embedded computing devices within the existing Internet infrastructure." That's tech-speak for machine-to-machine communication across the 'Net.

Do you have a smart phone? Then you're already part of the whole thing, whether you like it or not. Your cell phone is "uniquely identifiable" because of that little SIM card containing all your information, from other people's phone numbers to your own.

Do you have a smart refrigerator? No, I don't either, and I'm betting most people reading this don't. According to CNET.com, Samsung's version of the smart fridge cost upwards of $3,500 in June of 2014. That would be oh, about five times what the last refrigerator we bought cost us.

Now, if you just happen to own one of these smart fridges, and if you happen to have the right kind of phone (not an iPhone, in other words), you can make a call from your refrigerator. And see the day's headlines on the touch screen on your refrigerator. And play your TV on your fridge.

Does any of this make you want to get one? Only the true technophiles want to go this far.

The definition of a technocracy, per Google, is "control of society or industry by an elite of technical experts."

The mere fact I used my computer and went to Google to look it up is very much a symptom of how far technology has embedded itself in our lives. I no longer own a dictionary. Or a thesaurus. Or the Encyclopedia Britannica Remember those?

But I'm not here to inflict a conspiracy theory on you. I don't think we are actually a technocracy. Yet.

Why don't I think so? Because I just don't need to make a phone call from my refrigerator. And I can't imagine I ever will. Or that most of us ever will.

I know this is where the conspiracy theorist gets the little fleck of white foam near his mouth, mostly from the "uniquely identifiable" part of it. But wrapping foil around your head won't help. I do understand why it's scary.

When the federales know what's in my refrigerator, things may have gone too far.

But the point the conspiracy theorists miss out on is 99 percent of the decisions the technical elite are making aren't oriented on telling the feds whether I bought radishes or Brussel sprouts. They're to make lots and lots of money. From people who are willing to pony up thousands of dollars so they can make a phone call from their fridge.

Maybe it's a pipe dream, to believe we can disconnect ever again. I think we can, however, limit our participation, and keep it within reasonable bounds. I have a phone, a tablet and a laptop. One for contact, one for fun and family, one for work. No more.

But there are many, many other ways to give up information we inadvertently trip over. One of my guilty pleasures is frustrating big-city cashiers by saying "No," when they ask for my phone number. I had one youngster earnestly explain to me they don't ever actually use it. The ingenuousness of that statement staggered me. Of course they use it--that's my unique identifier.

One offshoot of the Internet of Things is to give those who sell products all the information on who, what and where you are. It will enable them to sell specifically to you.

Let's say you bought yourself a smart, battery-operated, buzzy toothbrush three months ago. Its planned obsolescence of 90 days is about to make it stop buzzing. This afternoon, an ad will pop up on your television, your computer and your phone, and keep popping up until you buy another. Or it will as long as you paid with your credit card, which carries your identifying phone number and address on its magnetic strip along with your credit card number, or, if you paid cash, if you told the cashier your phone number.

When you finally give in and buy the product again, your brand-new, version 2.0 toothbrush will now report to your dentist how often you brush, and tell the marketeers what kind of toothpaste you use.

But all is not lost. There really is a way to silence all the smart things we own.

Don't buy them.

I'm thinking out loud I just don't need some fink toothbrush ratting me out. My dentist will simply have to believe me.

And if you're doing something the feds could arrest you for, well, don't tell your fridge.

Politics, U.S. & world events

I don't write much about the larger events; it's actually one of the luxuries of writing for a weekly, community newspaper. I can ignore them most of the time.

Most of the time they're not funny, and I happen to like my world as lighthearted as I can keep it.

But on occasion, they stir me so much I simply can't stop my fingers typing until I've finished saying my piece.

They range from environmentalism to feminism to the tragedy of Charlie Hebdo to Michael Slager captured on video shooting Walter Scott in the back repeatedly on a sunny South Carolina day.

If they're here, it's because I felt very strongly about them. It does not mean my opinions necessarily match those of the general population.

Just saying.

Lisa C Hannon

Who guards the guardians

I did not want to write about this subject at all, but I ran across the video and I just couldn't look away as it began to play.

If you live under a rock, you may not have seen the news about South Carolina policeman Michael Slager shooting Walter Scott in the back as he ran away.

Scott was unarmed. In the video, Slager made no effort to actually run him down or chase after him, and Scott wasn't exactly breaking any landspeed records. Slager just kept walking, pulling the trigger again and again and again. Eight times, in all.

Maybe it was being raised in the Southwest, with the John Wayne virtues as part of what a man really was supposed to be—but a back shooter was far worse than a weasel; he was a lily-livered, yellow-bellied coward.

I still find Slager's calmness staggering, almost as if he'd gone through these actions in some scenario he'd played out in his head before. When he walked over to Scott's body and cuffed him, it was gut-wrenching. He did not check to see if the man was still alive. He just didn't want to know.

My sympathy for Scott's family knows no bounds. To lose someone you love to violence is tragic enough, but then to see his death replayed across the entire world.

Unimaginable.

It would have put me in a padded room.

Unfortunately, the abuse of power by those who guard the public safety is not a new one. It's at least as old as recorded language. In Latin, the phrase was "Quis custodiet ipsos custodes?" or "Who will guard the guardians?"

There are so many ripples of government response yet to come from the shooting that can't be predicted, but there are a few that can, including increased monitoring of police interaction with the public.

Some monitoring began more than a decade ago with dashcams in police cars.

They weren't put there to protect us, but to help stop serial lawsuits against law enforcement organizations accused of racial profiling.

The Department of Justice provided more than $21 million in federal assistance for installation of the dashboard cameras in the early 2000s. Currently, 72 percent of state and highway patrol vehicles have them.

Unfortunately, they actually had them in Ferguson, Missouri—but not the budget to get them installed.

When they work, they work well. A survey by the International Association of Police Chiefs showed complaints from taped traffic stops were withdrawn more than half the time when the person complaining was told the stop was on video.

Video of traffic stops also exonerated the officer 96.2 percent of the time and substantiated complaints only 3.8 percent of the remainder of those filed.

The survey found lots of unexpected outcomes, including increased officer safety, and increased unbiased eyewitness testimony, as incidents could actually be viewed in court by judge and jury.

Dashcams are obviously effective, but limited. Slager, for instance, was out of his car and off camera. Only the shots he took were audible. However, body-worn cameras are already in use by some police departments and their use is spreading.

For instance recently, officers in the Rialto, California, police department used body-worn cameras throughout the course of a year. Reported use of force by officers dropped by 60 percent, according to their chief of police.

Not just because of the officers' behavior. When the offenders knew they were on video, their behavior often quickly changed from the actions that got the law called on them to an attitude which didn't require forceful response.

Had Slager worn a body camera, would he have shot Scott in the back while he was running away? I just don't think so.

Scott's death is tragic without doubt. Does Slager's evil act justify spending millions nationwide for body-worn cameras on all law enforcement officers? No. The vast majority are dedicated, exceptional men and women who could never contemplate such an act.

But, if you think about 20 years of positive benefits to officers and the public from dashcams, and keep a weather eye, as did Rialto, on both sides—both law enforcement action and community reaction—then you might get a qualified "Yes."

Because I question everything, though, I was thinking out loud to my husband that body-worn cameras might be the precursor to Big Brother watching our every move.

He shrugged. "They can watch me all they want. The only ones who have to worry about it are the criminals."

And the evil ones.

Like Slager.

Who are you voting against?

There are some good things to be said about the apathy levels endemic to small town political scenes. If only one person runs for each office, at least you don't have to vote against anybody. The numbers of political "vote for me!" signs will be much fewer. And there won't be any hard feelings — something that is not necessarily a small thing in a small town.

But when you move to the national level, in considering the 2016 presidential election, are you as tired as I am of voting against people? Seriously, the last person I actually voted for was Ronald Reagan. Ever since then, I've pretty much voted against people. I might not have been particularly fond of the person running — but was either repulsed by or scared of the outcomes I could foresee from their opponent.

Now we get to the front runners for 2016. Throwback Thursday reigns supreme, as we are looking at the Bush dynasty and the Clinton camp, faced off yet one more time.

An old friend once said, "If you are crazy enough to want to run for any political office, then you are by definition insane, and I will not vote for you." I used to think he was a nutball. Ok, he was a nutball, but he had a point.

I finally have to concur with his statement, at least at the level of the office of the President of the United States. It is no longer "throwing your hat in the ring," it is "placing your posterior in the pressure cooker."

On that note, do you remember the epithet slung at Bill Clinton? "Slick Willie" was first used during his Arkansas political career, and clung to him throughout his presidency. He was laden with that nickname because, no matter what the subject ("It's according to what your definition of "is" is.") he could slither around it. Evidently, that rather interesting character defect was present early in his trajectory.

I'm no prognosticator, but as Hillary Clinton sidesteps her way around the State Department e-mail contretemps and the Benghazi biz, she is going to fully deserve the moniker of "Slick Hillie." I will bet you dollars to donuts she will come through without a scratch.

What I don't understand, and I'm thinking I never will, is why in the world she wants to run at all. This woman was put under every possible microscope, from every possible direction, and "stood by her man" (a phrase she ridiculed) while he was humiliated in every possible way. Watching the ravenous press slavering over his bones while the public cheered made Roman circuses look like small town carnivals. It was appalling to watch. Why would she do that again?

And Jeb Bush watched his father AND his brother age before their time while they stood on that mountaintop. What drives him to want to run this country?

I find myself harking back to the same thought—I'm uncomfortable with voting for either one of them, because the bottom line is, they are both crazy enough to want to be President.

And, of course, there are other things making me quite wary of either.

I just don't want to vote for another Bush. My memories of the Bush the First are pretty dim—but I've always been a little suspicious of a president who can't get re-elected for a second term. Considering our discomfort with change, we are quite addicted to the "devil-you-know" theory of re-election, in that we figure we at least know what's going to happen with the in-office goober, and don't want to risk whatever mayhem might ensue with a different one. And yet, he couldn't get elected for a second term.

Jeb's race will be forever tainted with the memories of Bush the Second, or as the much-lamented and sorely missed Molly Ivins always called him, "Shrub." I'm sorry if you loved him, but I will never be able to forget him standing on an aircraft carrier's deck, talking in front of people who were and would again be in harm's way, with a huge banner reading "Mission Accomplished" behind him. The vast majority of casualties we took in his war were after that speech.

I'm thinking out loud, even if Hillary Clinton is the right candidate, I'm not sure I can make it through another eight years of conspiracies, and shrouded communications, and Whitewater, and Benghazi. and blue dresses and on and on ad nauseam.

Paging General Colin Powell.

General Powell?

When someone hands you a bowl of ca-ca and says it's chocolate pudding, don't eat it

Since I voted for Ronald Reagan once upon a time, I must be a conservative, right? No, I always vote for the person when it comes to a presidential race. I am also not a liberal, but I know it's irritating that I won't step down on either side of that fence.

Here's the deal. In my opinion, the "us vs. them" thinking patterns are lethal — and people are paying the price. In the daily news right now is black vs. white, with more unrest and cops being shot in Ferguson, Missouri, and fraternity goober boys' racist chants.

Unfortunately, Ferguson isn't fixable with a few quips. It's going to take long, hard work on the part of a lot of people to help that situation.

But I'm thinking recent studies showing millennials approve of spanking their children might go a long way toward avoiding similar incidents to the fraternity mess. Unfortunately, we'll have to wait some 20 years down the road until this generation's offspring are in college. Maybe if the fraternidiots had been spanked as children for saying bad words, or doing something just because their brother told them to, we might have avoided that event in the first place.

And if you need more us vs. them thinking, there are always Democrats vs. Republicans. The Democrats are using the Republicans' filibuster tool against them, which is making the Republicans twitchy. Therefore, the Republicans are writing to foreign countries to let them know Obama has no power. Seriously? That's like letting people know Aunt Mabel's in the cracker factory again. Might be true, but you don't tell everyone. Just park her on the porch and let her rock, you know?

Then, of course, there's us vs. the Russians — OK, I'll give you that for one Russian, anyway. Vladimir Putin looks almost exactly like the boogie man that haunts my nightmares.

"Boo! Vee shall visit new-kew-lar vohr upon your fuzzy little head, you shtupid A-mare-uk-cain!"

And no, I have no idea why Putin sounds just like Colonel Klink from Hogan's Heroes. Not sure who generates the sound track for the villains in my nightmares.

And here's my favorite, all-time, takes the cake, slap-yo-mama, stop the presses argument.

Climate change. Did you just hear ominous music? Duh-duh-duh-DUH! They had to stop calling it "global warming," as the people up to their navels in snow find that annoying, but it's the same thing. What's interesting to me is we are no longer arguing about whether or not the climate is changing—now the us vs. them thinking is "humans are accelerating the problem" vs. "no we're not!"

I'm not arguing the climate is changing; I'm not even arguing whether or not humans are making it worse. How about we just stop debating it and start doing something about protecting human beings from the more disastrous effects?

You may notice, I did not say "protecting black people," or "protecting white people," from the effects of climate change. I said "protecting human beings." And, for you "animal parents" out there--that phrase makes me itch, but still--we can protect them too.

The thing is, until we stop the black/white, Democrats/Republicans, yes/no thinking, we don't have a snowball's chance in a West Texas summer of fixing anything. There are days when I despair of humans ever being able to hear an opposite viewpoint without foaming at the mouth.

There are exceptions. ISIS and Boko Haram come to mind. Negotiating with terrorists means everyone loses. Anyone who thinks differently is just not watching the news.

But in the more everyday run of things, those who can see both sides of an argument are called fence sitters. I'm often one of those, with the few noted exceptions. My fence is about two feet tall, easy to step over, padded quite nicely so I don't bruise myself, and has a swiveling seat to listen to both sides of the argument. That way, I'm comfortable until I hear something I can agree with, or at least nod and say, "You have a point."

Which drives my husband crazy.

I married a conservative. My family is conservative. I live in a conservative state. But I'm thinking out loud this doesn't mean I can stop thinking.

You shouldn't stop thinking either.

Don't just nod when someone puts a bowl of ca-ca on the table and tells you it's chocolate pudding.

Tell 'em it smells funny. And don't take a bite of it.

I am a woman, not a feminist

I am a woman, but I am not a feminist.

Don't start the celebration yet—or pull out the pitchforks to hunt me down. It's probably not for the reasons you think.

The biggest reason is because I think that, in identifying the battle as one of equal pay for equal work, my gender simply fought for the wrong thing. The forces of feminism took on the male definitions for what matters. Money. Power. Prestige.

It made women feel they must compete with men on men's turf, in men's terms, for what men value most. And it has left the battlefield littered with women who mourn because they fought the game by the boy's rules for what the boys want and they lost.

Fifty years later, a total of 53 Fortune 1000 companies have female CEOs. Just about one per year. That is not "winning" in anyone's estimation.

It was supposed to be about "choice," wasn't it? Feminism lost that battle when they made it clear what most women value simply doesn't matter. Go ahead, ask any stay-at-home mom whether she believes she has feminist backup for her choice.

Instead, most seem to feel guilty. For wanting to stay home with their children. How did this become a bad thing?

I am a woman and I do not want to be a CEO.

I have to qualify that--if I ever become a CEO, it will be because I started the company.

But I have zero desire to run a multinational, multi-billion-dollar mega-company.

Of course, they aren't exactly hunting me down to hand over the keys to the executive bathroom, either, so that works out pretty well.

Why don't I want it? For one thing, the very few women I've known who wanted those keys were not women I respected or trusted. They traded their humanity to become what they thought the company wanted.

To be fair, I've also met lots of male CEOs, as well as COOs, CFOs, CTOs, and other alphabet-soupy upper management.

I wouldn't invite most of them to dinner either. They have mostly sold their souls to the company store, and those people just don't interest me much.

I am a woman and I actually like men.

I think they're amazing—mostly in how much they are not like me. We don't think alike. This doesn't mean they're better than women or vice versa. We're simply different.

It's important to acknowledge that, respect that, and for me at least, to enjoy it.

I am a woman, and other than that one, I despise labels.

Labels are for pickle jars. My idea of myself, what I need, want, deserve or shouldn't have aren't expressible in a label. Nor are the needs and wants of all women.

To me, labels make conflict inevitable. As soon as a label like "feminist" shapes how you interact with those around you, it pushes those who don't feel the same way you do into behaviors that will inevitably result in discord.

Labels exclude much more than they ever include. "Feminism" leaves men out. By definition. Pretty sure men will stop wearing the "I'm a feminist" T-shirts when they stop getting women's attention with them.

I know feminists will say "You don't understand if you think it's only about equal pay." They're wrong. I understand it. I just think they fought the wrong fight.

Feminism should have celebrated the stay-at-home mothers as well as the female CEOs right to choose. Perhaps they could have chosen to make raising the next generation something men would fight to do, instead of fight to avoid.

But, by taking on business as the battleground instead, and restricting it to the men's world that was, women who strive for

CEO somehow feel they must assume male characteristics.

The flip side is that women (and men!) who choose to stay home are marginalized, made to feel like second-class citizens, unpaid, unsung, unloved, uncelebrated in a world that only values money. It was a mistake.

Feminists used "choice" to symbolize other things, but when you look at them, those choices completely prioritize business. Women still make less than men, dollar for dollar, at least partially because they must step out of their career trajectory to have children.

Why are we still fighting a battle that devalues us for perpetuating our species?

Once upon a time, I did not like being female.

Then I met and married my amazing husband and found out what being a woman, and a partner, actually means.

He does the cooking, because he's better at it. Is he a traitor to all men because he cooks?

He stinks at laundry, but will do it if I ask, and if I'm willing to have all my clothes look like they've been stored in Pringle's cans.

I bake bread, and do laundry. Am I a traitor to some cause I never espoused and never will?

I'm thinking out loud what we have here is a partnership, not a battleship. We don't feel the need to be on opposite sides.

Go ahead. Label that.

We have as much right to be here as the rest of the critters, you big goobers

I swear, if the extremists had their way, humans would crouch in their homes and never touch anything that might in any way affect any kind of life form other than our own.

Well, here's my opinion—we have just as much right to walk this earth as any of the flora and fauna that are out there, and I'm really getting tired of being told humans are only destroyers.

I was raised in rural East Texas, on 75 acres of pine woods. Half were old growth, half had been replanted, probably 20 years prior to us moving to the area. There was such incredible beauty in the old growth pines rooted in the red clay. Vines everywhere, little trickles of streams here and there, undergrowth so thick in most places you couldn't get through it.

There was also amazing beauty and order and strength in the replanted acres as well. Standing in one place, I could look down row after shady, green row of tall pines, guardians of a land where a tiny white-tail deer peered at me for a moment from around a tree trunk before bounding away.

The same thick carpet of pine needles that quieted my steps and allowed me to get so close to her made each of her sky-high jumps completely, eerily silent as she fled. It's an image imbedded in my mind still, decades later. Peace, strength, beauty and life, enabled by the hand of man, woven from nature's generosity.

I'm not saying we should change every inch of the landscape—but I am saying we are not a purely destructive force. We are a creative force, as well. If you've never driven down Glenwood Canyon in Colorado, I urge you to put it on your bucket list. It is breathtaking, not just for the natural scenery, but the highway that runs through it, which is an absolute marvel of human ingenuity and engineering.

Moving on to the fauna of this amazing world—one thing that bears remembering is that 99.9 percent of the species that have ever existed on this planet are now extinct. It is, apparently, part of the deal. Life is…ephemeral. One of the things that killed off many of those species was overspecialization.

See, the thing is, humans are omnivores. We will eat pretty much anything that isn't nailed down or red hot. Omnivores flourish in this world—from coyotes to cockroaches to, well, us.

On the flip side, animals that specialize don't survive.

For instance, the scientific opinion on why saber-toothed cats became extinct is that, when the large mammals they preyed on became scarce, they couldn't adjust to eat other food sources, or reduce their size to need less food. Their specialization, including the long fangs that helped them kill large prey, was their death sentence. Their departure, though, opened up space in the ecosystem for some of the mid-range cats, jaguars, cougars, and so on.

I'll let you draw the rest of the inference yourself.

I understand, well I stand as a witness at least, to the human drive to keep species from extinction, especially when we believe we're to blame.

But forests never allowed to burn grow so much undergrowth that, when the fire eventually comes along that can't be stopped, it destroys the forest completely. The over-thick undergrowth has become so much dry tinder feeding an unquenchable blaze.

Forests need occasional fires to clean the environment up, to stop the undergrowth from choking out trees and to add elements back to the soil. It took a long time for us to learn that fact.

Our suppression of natural forest fires ended up causing more harm than good. What if, by saving a species on its way to extinction, we are deterring or diminishing the chance of another species to take their rightful place in the environment? We may not be. But what if we are?

I'm not going to touch the whole question of climate change and our role in it or lack thereof.

I will note, however, when things are brought to our attention, we can change. Do you remember American highways 45 or 50 years ago? Litter was thick along every interstate. We changed that, particularly in Texas.

We're not perfect, but we are better.

Considering the evidence of tsunamis, volcanoes, earthquakes and meteor impact craters, the Earth may well swat us someday much like we would swat a fly.

But I'm thinking out loud we have as much right to be here as any other critter until that happens.

And if we are the ones who caused all this, we are also the only ones at this point who can fix it. So let's get to fixing, people.

What purpose did Charlie Hebdo's satire serve? What did their deaths accomplish?

This piece was originally published in a community newspaper. Most community papers will not make mention of the tragic shootings in France—where terrorists gunned down 10 of the editorial staff of Charlie Hebdo, a satirical news organization, and two policemen. You may have seen references elsewhere to "Je Suis Charlie," (I am Charlie).

The ostensible purpose of the murderers was to punish the news magazine's mockery of Mohammed and the Islamic religion, especially graphic cartoons of the prophet.

The editors of Charlie Hebdo poked the already-enraged bear that is radical Islam, and now their families, as well as many others, have to find a way to live without them.

People make choices and die for them every day. The terrorists made their choices and ended up dead, but not before they took even more lives—of people who did not make the choices Charlie Hebdo made.

Our military members choose to protect the freedoms we often take for granted, including freedom of religion, speech and the press, including the ability to write and publish satire.

But there is a question, often shoved to the side in the emotional aftermath. Does freedom of the press mean you publish absolutely everything?

I ask because I've taken the easy way out once before. I chose to stop writing these articles almost four years ago because I felt I couldn't say the truth, even with a dose of humor. Had I written about what was happening at work at that time, I would have probably been fired—and indeed, ended up leaving that job only a few months later.

Fortunately, years of distance from those events helps diminish them. I chose not to publicize my petty little truths to keep me, my family and people I genuinely cared about from being hurt.

My choice not to write about my tempest in a teapot was because I couldn't come up with any good writing about it would accomplish. It would not have diminished the corporation's reputation, especially considering the fact they had already laid off the equivalent of 15 percent of the town's population. I chose not to write, because in my best personal judgment, it was not to anyone's benefit for me to do so.

I don't mean to compare my tiny concerns to the tragedy of the murderous rampage in France.

What it did give me however, was experience which leads me to ask—what did their satire accomplish besides their deaths? What did they think taunting radical Islam and Islamists would achieve?

I have poked at the question every way I know, and I simply can't come up with a good answer. They were already under police guard, and those law enforcement officers died with them. No one seemed to have asked themselves the question, "What purpose will this action serve?"

The people who publish community newspapers ask themselves these questions, and make choices every single publication day.

Drawing once again from my own experience, I knew I would never be a big-city journalist when I served as the managing editor of a community paper in Central Texas at the beginning of this millennium.

On my way to work one morning, there was a wreck in the town square. A little 70-year-old lady was sitting on the curb bawling, and the police were already there. I took a couple pictures of her car sitting halfway into the shattered store front. When I got closer, I realized she was the manager.

I sat down beside her, put my arm around her shaking shoulders, and asked if she was OK. She nodded, though tears were still trickling down her face. Her first coherent words were "Mama's going to be so mad!" Her 90-year-old mother owned the store.

After she calmed down, she asked me not to put the pictures in the paper. As a newsperson, they were news. But, as a community newsperson, I knew everyone in town would know it had happened long before the paper came out the next Wednesday. No pictures ran with the short piece that I buried on 2A a week later.

Look, that was small community doings, and radicalized Muslims are affecting the world. I get it.

And I also understand the human spirit that reacts to threats of reprisal by saying, "If we don't publish, the bad guys win." Were this world perfect, Charlie Hebdo would have been published without bloodshed and tragedy.

But what did their deaths accomplish? What were the cartoons meant to accomplish? Turn someone away from radical religious belief?

I was raised around what a lot of people would term fairly extremist religious beliefs, and I'm here to tell you — they do not have a sense of humor. They have a sense of anger. And publishing those cartoons did nothing but get themselves and a bunch of innocent bystanders killed.

I'm thinking out loud that, just because you can publish something doesn't always mean you should.

She's Thinking Out Loud

Holidays

Holidays got a lot more special for me after I remarried—during my first marriage, they were often spent hundreds or thousands of miles away from home and family. That said, as you'll find out in some of the pieces that follow, holidays at home in East Texas had their special little hazards.

When the kids can get home—not always a possibility in a military family—holidays now mean the patter of little feet (and big ones). And when they can't, we go somewhere else. Works for us.

Sometimes my mind did change, as on the subject of New Year's resolutions—but then again, it's a woman's prerogative, right?

Right.

Dear Santa, I really wanted those Rock'em Sock'em Robots

Dear Santa,

I just wanted to remind you of all those years ago, when I was tiny and my mother would take my letters to Santa, read them and tell me she was checking them for spelling, and then burn them in the fireplace so the smoke would take them to the North Pole. Smart lady.

I never did get the Rock 'Em Sock 'Em Robots I was asking for.

I've forgiven you for that, but seriously, I'm thinking you owe me. And I've been pretty good this year.

So here's my top five Christmas list.

First and foremost, would you at least think about bringing peace on earth, goodwill to men, women, children and dogs this year?

I'm figuring cats don't care, as long as there's a can of tuna and a can opener.

Second, I think I've already mentioned the daughter who's in Army technical school now. Just bring her home safe from wherever they send her. I worry, you know.

Third, I'd like a stepstool, please, one that's about a foot tall. That way, when I'm chastising my six-foot-something son, I can look him in the eye. Being patted on the top of your head when you're in full flood is demoralizing.

Fourth, I want someone to make out all these Christmas cards lurking on my kitchen table, yelling at me to get them finished and get them out of here.

Fifth? Well, I can't think of a fifth thing. I have everything else I've ever wanted, a family of my own, a husband who thinks I'm gorgeous, or is willing to say so, which amounts to the same thing, a house, food on the table, at least seven dollars in the bank, maybe as much as ten. It's been an amazing year, full of joy and laughter, major triumphs and minor tragedies, friends, family, and fun.

Thank you very much.

Lisa

I find I can't resist the opportunity to think out loud about what Christmas is for me. You should know up front I understand the reason for the season, and probably know more about the history of the celebration than your average Josephine.

Christmas for me, though, is inextricably tangled with memories of my mother. The grief I felt after her death shut my spirit down for a number of years.

I found I could not celebrate even the most celebrated of births when all I could feel was my loss.

When I lost her, I lost Christmas, too.

So many people close to me have lost much-loved parents this year, and I grieve for and with them.

The first sign I was beginning to emerge from that dark place was when I began to feel I could once again survive a little Christmas joy.

It's OK not to feel like celebrating, and you don't have to force yourself into something you don't feel. But please know, when I could love Christmas again, when I finally brought it back into my life, I found part of Mama inside me.

She is the part of me that loves giving. My mother seriously thought about Christmas all year long. I never went shopping with her, ever, that I didn't hear her say at some point, "Oh, your Aunt Billie would love that," or "Your sister would love that little knick-knack thing." If she had the funds, whether it was a quarter or a dollar or however much, she would buy it.

We found stuff stashed from one end of the house to the other when she died, all wrapped, and much of it labeled for the receiver.

Her generosity of spirit was more than just about gifts, though. It was amazing, life-changing.

I asked her once why she let one of my brothers put his electricity bill in her name. He was behind in his bills, and the power company wouldn't turn it on for him. She just looked at me and blinked, and said, "I'd do the same for you."

And that is what Christmas means to me: A spirit of unquestioning, unfettered giving that comes from the heart.

My mother's spirit.

My 16-year-old just e-mailed me a link to his wish list last night. Can't set it on fire and send it to Santa at the North Pole, because I'm pretty sure it would melt my microchips.

But I'm thinking out loud it really is one more opportunity to prove my mother's Christmas spirit lives forever in my heart.

It must be, because I'm seriously contemplating putting down cold, hard cash for item number seven on my son's wish list: "The Zombie Survival Guide."

Hope your Christmas is very scary, um…merry, too.

My homesick soldier daughter is on my mind on Independence Day

July 4th is over; the fireworks were outstanding. I went up to the Coliseum for a while to assist the Chamber, but gladly came home and watched the fireworks from my back porch. You could feel the crrrummpp of the fireworks mortars all the way to my house on the other side of town.

The thumping mortars made me think of the Army, and my homesick soldier daughter sitting in a land far, far away. It is so tough, having her so far away, but I truly believe this experience will be a large part of the amazing woman she's going to become. This is part and parcel of that strength that it takes to be part of the military. It is almost unexplainable.

But then, I'm a writer, I have to try.

There is something about wanting something so desperately, like coming home, and knowing you cannot have it, that begins to distill the strength of your heart.

The people you work next to are in the same position as you — aching for home, scared sometimes, happy sometimes, but with the underlying sense of just not wanting to be where you are and knowing you can't change it: their determination adds to your strength as well.

You and the person sitting next to you at work and the soldier marching next to you in formation, you all have to stand up under your burden, you cannot falter. People are depending on you to be where you are.

Each realization reminds you once more you are in a place you cannot leave, doing a job which must be done. It purifies your strength a little further, and layers a coat of Kevlar around your bruised heart. That armor holds it together, until, for just a few moments on the phone to home, you can be a child again, in the privacy of your room.

Every day you're away, though, refines and sharpens the armor-piercing stiletto of homesickness. You are on the other side of the world, and the only thing that makes it feel any better is you're going home on leave. At the same time, it makes it worse, because it's such a long time before you go home. Even it's only a week away, a week is way too long!

When you do go home, everything is the same, and nothing. It's not the same place you left, even if they kept your room without changing it. It's so hard to sort out why, but you finally realize the house didn't change, your family didn't change. The parents are a little grayer and your siblings are taller, but they're the same people you left. You changed.

It's the same for every child who comes home from college or any life-changing experience, but for the military son or daughter, you have to mature faster, better, stronger, further and harder. So the disconnect between who you are now and who you were such a short time ago is vastly wider.

We parents are left looking at this person we are sure we love, but we don't really know you anymore. On the phone, over e-mail, on Facebook, you're still ours. But this thin, smiling grown-up who walks in our house in uniform is a stranger who just looks like our child. The soft edges have worn off, been sharpened by experience. You are ours, still, but you've become your own and so much more, in some way we cannot define.

In honor of Memorial Day, a Rotary Club member ran the video from Saving Private Ryan where all the boats with all the soldiers landed. They ran onto the beach and straight into the German guns. By a few minutes into the presentation, I had my hands over my eyes, and shortly thereafter put my fingers in my ears so I couldn't hear the screams.

I'm thinking out loud I will not be watching any war movies anytime soon. At least until my daughter comes home.

Maybe never.

Making resolutions for other people is so much easier

Fifty percent of us make New Year's resolutions each year. Of those resolutions half of us make, according to Psychology Today, 88 percent of them fail.

It's true from my own experience, as well. I managed a fitness center for a bit. The owner told me 80 percent of their subscriptions were bought in January of each year, and of those new clients, 8 of 10 never showed up again after February. She was absolutely right.

I don't make resolutions for myself, haven't for years. I think I'm going to start making resolutions for other people instead. That avoids all the angst when things don't work out, you know? Plus I get to point fingers at someone besides the one in the mirror.

You should try it. There's a tremendous satisfaction in making resolutions for other people. Holding them to it... well, that's just a whole 'nother conversation.

For our son: Your resolution is to call your parents once a month, whether you feel a tremendous need to do so or not. Seriously. I understand you genuinely prefer to text. However, if the only time we hear your voice is when someone's pregnant or someone's dead, we start to twitch every time the phone rings.

For our daughter: Your resolution is to eat right, exercise gently, and do everything you possibly can to have a healthy, happy little girl (or boy, just in case they were wrong!) in April. And, because you are an amazing soldier, to do all the soldier stuff to your usual high standards while you are hugely pregnant. Because that's what you do.

You also resolve to have the baby on my birthday, because you know it would make me very, very happy. It would also make it a lot easier for her grandpa to remember her birthday, as that is not his strong suit.

For our grandson: Your resolution is to remember us when we only see you once or twice a year, because that makes us old people get all choked up. I know you're only three years old, so I'll keep it simple this year.

Starting next year, though, we need to talk about the fact your granddaddy and I don't want to end up in an old folk's home. That means it's going to be your job to talk your mama out of it when the time comes. There's a savings bond in it for you.

For my best friend in the whole wide world: You, my dear, will resolve to take a deep breath and lift your head up from the wedding planning for your baby girl and call me at least once a week. We will talk, and I will commiserate, and then we will all be glad when August comes and goes and the wedding of the century is finally over.

For Mr. Barack Obama: You just need to resolve to do nothing more in the your lame duck years to lead to "the infamous" being used in front of your name when your presidency is cited in the history books.

For the Congress of these United States: Y'all aren't listening, so I'm not even going to waste the ink to write down a resolution for you. Talk about falling on deaf ears.

For the people who put pictures in the cloud: To those of you who are putting nekkid pictures of yourself in electronic storage on the Internet, and then getting upset because someone else sees them. It's time you make a resolution that, if it would embarrass you if your mama saw it, then don't take pictures of it. And if you can't do that, then don't upload them online. Anywhere. A little common sense for the electronic age would go a long way.

There are an awful lot of other things I can't even try to be funny about, especially with the media flooding us with protest images from both sides of the police shootings. It sure would be great if we could all resolve just to stop the hating and start some healing.

But whatever else happens, each new year begins fresh as the new-fallen snow, untouched, pristine and ready to be lived.

Hope takes a breath and begins again as the calendar starts anew on Jan. 1. We sure could use a little hope.

And on that note.

For my husband: You need to resolve to change nothing, because I'm thinking out loud I love you just the way you are.

Anything starting, "You know what your problem is?" probably won't end well

My first attempt at this article was a list of New Year's resolutions for other people, and I realized I was doing something I purely despise when someone does it to me.

Anything starting, "You know what your problem is?" is probably not going to end well.

As long as you're reasonably sane and not into anything wickedly weird, it should apply, right?

I mean, if you want a bunch of neon-blue weasels to paint your toenails pink while you're eating a snow cone, I'm thinking that may not be what your next-door neighbor's into, so even with the Golden Rule, a teensy bit of restraint is demanded.

So, that's decided.

My number one resolution for the upcoming year is to attempt to treat others as I would like them to treat me. Except for the weird stuff. No, I'm not listing my weird stuff, go look for your own.

This article is putting my first resolution into action. Anyone who writes resolutions for me will probably get a dirty look minimum.

Getting a running start at my second resolution, I have to ask a question. Have you ever made a to-do list and put something on there you've already completed? Makes you feel better about your list, you know, when you see something already done.

So with that in mind, I'm thinking my second resolution will be to read at least two books a week. Considering I usually get through three or four that makes one resolution I'm fairly sure I can keep.

My third resolution is a little harder. I'm thinking I need to stop letting myself get annoyed by non-important things. As a friend once told me, "Don't sweat the petty things, and don't pet the sweaty things." Of course, sweaty is a whole lot easier to diagnose than petty. If it won't matter by this time next year, I'm thinking it's not terribly important, though.

Fourth, I need to stop questioning good things. An old business partner of mine once told me, "When everything's going right.... Stop arguing!" I was blessed so much from so many different directions last year, and I guess I feel I don't deserve it, or it won't last.

Fifth one is right along those same lines. I need to tone down the worrying. And, see number four, I worry just as much about the good things as I do about the bad things.

Resolution number six is to ignore and actively avoid any emotional vampires that show up. That's what I call those folks who seem to get their jollies creating negative feelings, stirring up controversy, finding drama where there is none, trading on gossip and secrets and lies.

These people seem to thrive on flinging bad stuff around like a monkey in the zoo flinging poo. Well, shoo! No room at the inn for you. The rhymes were accidental. Really.

Seventh and final resolution is to set smaller goals to reach larger changes.

I'm thinking out loud I need to set reasonable, achievable, interim goals for a lot of things. Like losing weight at a rate of a pound a week, rather than a pound a day. Or getting taller. I'm thinking if I can get just an eighth of an inch taller each year, in ten years, I'll be five foot three!

Disclaimer: All the resolutions listed above are neither those of the management nor the publishers of the document which you hold in your hand.

I sincerely hope next year is peaceful, prosperous and purposeful for you and yours, and you are not troubled with vampires and suchlike.

Don't be a horse's butt at Christmas. And no skipping.

I'm in a Christmas-ish mood, because I have been wrapping presents all day long. With only two weeks left, the agony is nearly over anyway.

While I've been trundling around buying gifts, wrapping them, and thinking about what to make for the holiday dinner, I've been wrapped up in my memories of other Christmases in other years. Not necessarily wonderful memories, at least not all of them.

I was a military wife for nearly three decades, and there were a number of years the holidays found me cooking for just me and the now-ex-husband, hundreds and occasionally thousands of miles away from my mother's home in Texas.

While I usually wasn't there, I certainly got to hear about it.

For instance, there was the one year my mother called me in Montana and told me she had just burned all the Christmas decorations because one of my brother's wives had said something awful about my mother not actually being part of her family. That was a two-hour phone call.

That may have been the year Mama started handing out the little trophy of the north end of a southbound horse. The family called it "The Horse's Butt of the Year" award, and it was awarded mostly in theory, and in jest, but occasionally in reality. Whoever showed their posterior the most for the holidays was the recipient. Again, at least in theory.

One year, that same sister-in-law won the trophy for making me cry. I was listening to the Mormon Tabernacle Choir sing Christmas Carols on the radio while I was cooking at Mama's.

She came in, turned the radio off and told me listening to heathen idol-worshippers meant I would burn in hell for all eternity. Made Mama mad, thus the trophy award ceremony.

Another year it was one of the nephews' girlfriends, who kept going around showing all the guys her tattoo. I'm pretty sure it was my sister who came in completely wall-eyed, saying "I just about slapped that thing back in her bra!" I'll leave the rest to your imagination. Not sure that was actually Christmas, but it was certainly at my mother's house.

And that's what happens after all these years. All the holidays start to blend together, and the pictures seem to be the reality, or the memory I have is of a picture, and not real at all.

Christmas at my in-laws was always interesting, as well, although there were no actual trophies awarded.

One year, my mother-in-law took me to task and then started slamming things around in the kitchen because I had "put the butter in the butter dish wrong." Still haven't figured that one out like 25 years later.

I'm tempted to forgive her due to holiday stress, but thank goodness, she's an ex-mother-in-law, so I don't have to do anything with her at all.

Holiday stress hits all of us. For instance, I know I'm putting too much pressure on myself and those around me if I go around expecting Christmas to be perfect. It isn't, and it never will be.

However, this Christmas, for the very first time in my life, I will have my own children around me. We'll probably open gifts on Christmas Eve, since their dad will be leaving for work at 6:30 in the morning on Christmas Day.

My daughter will be home from her Army technical school, and we will have our son with us this year as well—last Christmas they were both at their birth mother's in Colorado, but this year, they'll be here. Last year, we weren't married yet. This year, we are.

This may be the last time we get to have both of them around, at least for a while. There is no way of knowing yet where Kelsey will be stationed next Christmas. I don't care where she is, as long as she's safe, and as long as we can hear from her once in a while.

Fear for her safety has all been put aside for a little while, in order to simply revel in the joyous place my life has become.

Joy for me is a spiraling thing, flying upwards into the clear, chilly nights, like sparks flying upward from a fire. I want to hug my entire life to me, and sing Christmas carols, and skip.

OK, maybe not skip.

However, considering that, when I saw my daughter the day after Thanksgiving, I completely surprised myself by bursting into tears, I'm afraid the chances I will rain a tear or two on Christmas Day are very high.

We've saved putting up the tree and decorating until she comes home, the thought of which made her shed a tear or two as well.

I'm thinking out loud I should have bought a few more boxes of tissues, 'cause we're probably both going to get a little soggy.

I can't wait for Christmas!

Thanksgiving was awesome, and Jesus won the war on Christmas

My family celebrated Christmas on Thanksgiving night—I basically just used it as an excuse to give gifts to the people I love. I loved watching my people open a few small, simple gifts, especially the three-year-old grandson.

We won't be together at Christmas, so it seemed appropriate to celebrate while I had all my chickens under one roof. It seldom happens when your offspring are all military, so I took shameless advantage.

Unlike most of the U.S., I work in a virtual workplace, so I no longer suffer under the self-imposed obligation of making sure everyone who works with me gets a card with a scribbled signature.

I do make sure to send out an e-mail with warm wishes before I sign off the computer for the holiday. Sort of an e-Christmas wish, if you like.

My husband, thank goodness, is a guy, so it just won't occur to him to give Christmas cards out to all the other guys he works with. Luckily, it won't occur to them, either, so that works out fine for everybody.

The first Christmas we were together, I wrote all his workplace greeting cards up myself, and handed them to him to deliver. That was the last time.

This year, for any number of reasons, including the move from one house to another on the ranch, and a Thanksgiving house full of people, I also never quite got it together enough to print and send the usual fifty-plus photo cards. I didn't miss doing it at all. This may be the break I needed to finally stop killing trees for Christmas—at least in terms of the paper used for greeting cards, anyway.

So, whether I willed it or no, life has streamlined the holiday for me—and I'm really OK with that.

I also don't get too het up about what it's called, so in terms of the whole "Can we still say 'Merry Christmas?'" thing and separation of church and state, and what the heck we're supposed to say now, I don't worry about it too much either way.

Stuff like that really did bother me once upon a time. A Walmart greeter handed me a carnation one May Sunday, saying "Happy Mother's Day!" and I handed it back to him, telling him quite sharply I wasn't anybody's mother.

It wasn't his fault I'd gotten some bad news from the fertility specialist just a few months prior. What I should have done was take it in the spirit it was given. Belated apologies, sir, and I hope I didn't scar you for life.

That all changed, of course, when I got a son and daughter as part of the amazing package that came along with my marriage to Corey some years ago. They both call me "Mom," which made my Grinch-ish little heart grow five sizes, at least.

Add to that the fact grandson number one, who calls me "Gramily," is about to be joined by granddaughter number one in April.

I can't wait to have a little girl to spoil and make much of, along with the little boy who found his place in my heart before he even learned to walk. Every little voice that calls me anything resembling "Grandma" just makes my poor, battered heart grow one more size.

These marvelous people's entry into my life, along with their father, initiated enormous changes in the way I thought about, well everything—but most especially about holidays.

Out of respect for those who still worry, though, it might reassure you to know the Washington Post ran an article just a few days back titled, "The War on Christmas is Over. Jesus Won."

One of the surveys they quoted showed Americans, four to one, prefer "Merry Christmas," and even non-religious Americans prefer it three to one.

So, from me and my family, to the first seven of you, "Merry Christmas!" And to the other two, "Happy Holidays!"

Observe the holiday in whatever way you prefer. Call it whatever you like. Worship how you want—the freedom to do so is a right my children and every other U.S. soldier, sailor, airman and marine is out there to preserve.

Most of them can't be home for this holiday. Please spare a thought or prayer for them.

We're thinking out loud we hope you have the happiest of holiday seasons. However you celebrate, we hope it's filled with love, laughter, family, food, friends and fun.

She's Thinking Out Loud

Lisa C Hannon

Texas

Other than my family, both close and extended, Texas is probably my greatest love. One of the biggest joys of my life is that, in the many adventures my life has held, I've gotten to travel over the depth and breadth of it, from the Panhandle to Brownsville, from Texarkana to El Paso to Orange, to the Big Bend Country, and hundreds of small towns in between.

I write with a Texas accent because I speak with a Texas accent. My parents were both Texans, and though I was born elsewhere, we were here every summer and finally settled permanently when I was six in Nacogdoches County in East Texas.

As of this book's publication, I am fortunate enough to live on a ranch in West Texas, where my husband is responsible for the hunting and ranching fleet, from pickup trucks to hunting buggies, dirt bikes to bulldozers to cattle trailers and lawnmowers. He's a busy man— because in the desert, if it has moving parts, it breaks!

I don't know if I'll live here 'til I die.

But I know I'll always be a Texan.

Transplant sees the beauty in the West Texas desert

OK, here's my dirty little secret.

I'm a foreigner.

Oh, don't get your knickers in a knot, I'm not from another country, I'm just from across the state, over in East Texas. I grew up in the middle of one of the last great forests of the United States, the Piney Woods.

Most of my childhood was spent midway between Looneyville and Lilbert, near Nacogdoches, the town with the arguable claim to be "The Oldest Town in Texas." If you ever studied Texas history, you probably heard of it.

Saying the environment was different in East Texas than it is in the western part of the state undervalues what "different" means. It was rolling hills, winding red dirt roads, creeks, rivers, pine trees, hayfields and lush, green countryside. Lack of water was seldom the problem, more the reverse—too much water, as in floods and ice storms, 95 percent humidity that makes 95 degrees feel like 125. It was more like drinking air than breathing it, often enough. And I loved it. It was my home.

I traveled through West Texas only on the way to somewhere else, living in Nevada,

Colorado, Montana, even in Europe a few times.

In 2007, I came here to West Texas to visit my sister, and then drove up through New Mexico, Colorado, Wyoming, and all of Montana. Perching up near the Canadian border, looking back through the drive, West Texas pulled at me.

A year later, when my old life blew up, I came here without a whole lot more than my clothes and my car. Moved in with family, found a job, began to get involved with the community. Reluctantly at first, as it had never been my style before, but eventually with enthusiasm.

West Texas threw its figurative arms around me, teaching me about the area history, how things work and who makes them work. In every spare moment, I drove. Down to Big Bend, out to Balmorhea, up to the Guadalupe Mountains, through Crane and Girvin, Imperial and Grandfalls and Royalty. Up to Monahans and Kermit, across to Alpine, to Fort Davis, Sanderson, Marathon, Terlingua. And first, foremost and always, Fort Stockton.

This country wrapped my heart around it. I have marveled at what the cursed dust creates at sunrise and sunset—incredible shades of red flooding more than half the sky dome above.

I have seen a double rainbow stretch across the plateaus, arched between two lowering clouds, while the sun still shines on me. I have seen the land bloom from a few days of precious rain, shades of citrine and amethyst wildflowers and blood red ruby cactus flowers coloring the landscape, fading moments later to the sepia tones of the desert, shrouding themselves with the dust to survive the sun until the next rains come.

I miss the rains of East Texas sometimes. There is such beauty here, though, of a kind I've found nowhere else. And, I found the love of my life in West Texas, a transplant like me.

It's easy to point out issues, and the lack of this, that or the other thing. There are problems here, like there are problems everywhere. But I won't apologize for loving it here—after all, I'm just thinking out loud.

Plant homicide and the price of pecans

It was such a pleasure driving back from Missouri to see the carpets of tiny purple and yellow wildflowers everywhere across Texas. Then when I got home to the ranch, just in the week I was gone, they'd sprung up here as well.

The final sign of spring is also here at my house—I bought flower seeds.

I'm so looking forward to getting my hands dirty preparing some flower pots to put out in the front of the house. I'll plant those seeds, water them faithfully and wait eagerly to see the first green shoots. Then I'll enjoy the blooms all spring and summer long.

OK, that whole paragraph was pretty much a lie.

I don't like dirt under my fingernails, so I'll wear gloves while I get those flower pots prepped and shove seeds into the soil. I will plant far too many seeds in them, because I always do. It's kind of my tiny version of "survival of the fittest." I have this idea they're elbowing each other under the surface of the dirt, trying desperately to emerge into the light of the sun.

They will immediately regret it, because then the West Texas sun will fry their poor little green carcasses.

This will be because I will mostly forget about watering them until I walk by and the dirt looks like the surface of Death Valley at high noon, cracked and broken. Then I'll flood the poor seedlings with water until they blub-blub for mercy.

After alternating drought and drowning for a month or so, about half of what I planted will come up anyway, 'cause life is a persistent little critter, and will often win out over even my treatment.

However, due to the overall trauma, most of what survives will be spindly and trembly, except for one three-foot-tall flower that is horribly ugly. I will name it Hannibal, and it will be healthy as all get out. It will wave at me sarcastically all spring and summer long. Meanwhile, it's painfully thin and sickly cousins below it will droop and wilt and look all dramatically neglected. Which they are.

Eventually, the extremely healthy weeds will cover those stunted little flowers up so you can't see them anymore. Hannibal, on the other hand, will have to be evicted with a big shovel, burned, and then his ashes buried at a crossroads with a stake through them to get him to quit coming back.

So why do I do it? Because it's spring in Texas!

And because at some point, my husband will stop asking pointed questions about me watering the flowers and start watering them himself. Because he loves me. I think that's why, anyway.

Unlike me, he is proof that hope truly springs eternal. Wherever we have been, in the six years we have been together, my husband has planted fruit trees every spring. Because of our peripatetic adventures, however, we have yet to be there when they're old enough to bear fruit. Well, other than those spindly little first two or three that you have to pinch off and get rid of so the tree can concentrate on growing.

He's already planted this year's fruit trees — but this time, we have no reason to go elsewhere, and plan to be here canning peaches and pears from them next year. He's also starting a couple apple trees from seed in a cup on the kitchen window sill. The man truly believes he will be able to get an apple tree to bear fruit in West Texas.

There is something quite endearing about that — and considering my distinct lack of horticultural skills, I have no room to talk about what will and won't grow anywhere, so I'll shut up now. He also bought peppers, green beans and tomatoes to plant, none of which I'll eat.

Now we have to decide if we're past the last frost. I sure hope so, because we have pecan trees, apricots, figs and a few trees of unknown potential here.

Their potential is unknown because in mid-March last year, we had an ice storm where ice coated everything for days. Every fruit and nut-bearing tree on this side of the ranch lost their leaves and spent the next few weeks naked and shivering. None bore fruit all year except a few fig trees.

If we escape without a frost, I'm thinking out loud I'd be willing to pick up some pecans off the ground, shell them and freeze them.

Especially when they're more expensive by the pound than a T-bone steak.

Tap dancing with the Texas tree roaches

Remember how ready I was for spring? Well, I'm getting my springtime, but it sure is mixed with a big old whopping dose of summer. It's like a collage of days—a little spring peeking out from behind the days that hit a hundred degrees. A thunderstorm last night leads to a hot and sweaty day today.

The trees we planted are sure liking it—all but two. The fig tree we brought with us from the last house couldn't take another re-planting, I guess. It turned into a fig stick, without even enough energy to fall over.

One of the plum trees gave up the ghost, too. The rest of the fruit trees all tried to bear some kind of fruit. My husband mourned 'cause he had to take off those first baby fruits to let the tree grow. We are not patient people, we Hannons.

The bamboo's growing like mad along the back fence. At this rate, by next spring, we're going to have to put up a block to keep it from taking over the yard. The tomatoes and jalapeno peppers are very happy, too.

What passes for a lawn in back and front is certainly growing, but I'm not sure it's grass. In fact, I'm absolutely sure it's not grass. All the weeds we killed earlier in the year came back, and brought their friends.

My husband and I made an agreement. If it's green, and the mower will cut it down, it's part of the lawn. Looks a little bumpy when it's growing out, but looks great when you've just cut it.

The humidity is genuinely great for the plants, as was that little spot of rain on Sunday. I, however, went for a mile walk this morning, and felt like I was trying to breathe swamp air.

I've gotten used to our desert dryness, and forget what it's like to breathe any kind of humidity. I grew up in East Texas, which is almost sub-tropical this time of year, so you'd think I could take it, but am apparently conditioned now to our dry sauna climate.

Unfortunately, the flies and the bugs love the humidity even more than the plants. That said, I never could figure out why they decide to come inside the house, away from the outsideness.

For instance, we had our first big old, Texas-sized tree roach of the year, crawling along the living room wall, waving his feelers around in a very menacing fashion.

You know what I'm talking about — those big cockroach-looking things that look like they're on steroids and weight lifting out back in between cupboard raids. If they could talk, they'd sound like Arnold Schwarzenegger, saying "I'll be back." Well, that one won't be back.

Those of you who know me know I'm not exactly a big old girly-girl. I wear jeans and boots all the time, short haircut, semi-no-nonsense, pretty businesslike.

Well, that would be until I see a big old bug. I can get downright hysterical, standing on a chair doing a tap dance if I catch sight of a cockroach.

Or a spider. Spiders scare the snot out of me.

That's OK—I'm married to a big strong man, and he's willing to kill bugs for me.

Especially moths. He hates moths. Not sure why, but I really don't care.

If they're in the house, they're fair game. If they stay outside, I generally don't hire a hitman.

Luckily, the boy caught sight of the evil too-many-legged thing and warned his dad. They haven't seen me completely wigged out yet, and I'm thinking out loud we can all just wait on that particular experience.

Of course, they don't see me most of the time when I'm walking, and the lizards and I make each other jump about a foot and a half and take off in opposite directions.

I don't mind that so much, kind of getting used to it. Gets my heart rate up, I can even pretend I'm trying to add a little cardio burst into my walking routine, you know?

First time I see a snake, though, I'm thinking out loud I'll be finding a treadmill and walking inside where it's air conditioned.

Snakes don't like treadmills.

What does a northern rodent know about West Texas weather anyway?

My husband is just itching to start planting stuff, and the weather won't cooperate.

The folks that owned the house before us evidently didn't believe a front lawn was necessary for their happiness, so it was mostly weeds and dirt. We killed all the weeds, but now we're left with dirt. There is the occasional optimistic blade of grass here and there. We want to plant grass seed, but if it freezes, it will kill it, and the weather-critters still keep saying there's at least one more cold snap headed our way like a freight train.

Went out and picked out a whole bunch of flower bulbs to plant, because the folks at Wal-Mart headquarters were apparently as optimistic as my husband. They've been selling them for weeks now. I refuse to plant them and then have to go dig 'em right back up and bring 'em back in the house.

We have planted a couple of trees we bought at the tree sale benefiting the USDA local programs. They look very shivery and reproachful at the moment, and I can tell they would rather be inside the house in a pot or something, but that is just not going to happen.

The fig tree, well, fig bush at this point, we brought with us from our last place is bravely putting out buds. It got stripped of everything in the end-of-summer hailstorms last year, so it's pretty traumatized. Hopefully it will survive.

I tend to use that phrase a lot where plants are concerned. My ex-husband told me once he felt like an accessory to murder every time he bought me a house plant.

I just call it a policy of benign neglect. If they can't cope with being ignored, unwatered and unloved, they aren't going to make it.

As a direct result, I couldn't get anything green to survive for a number of years. Finally got a pothos, you know, like the ones people have that climb all over their bookcases? It survived for about six months, and then we moved. Killed it.

My current husband's a lot more optimistic than I am about the survival rates for everything. Of course, he's the one who waters the aloe vera in the living room once a week. Unlike my ex, he's smart enough to take the responsibility for plant survival away from me completely. That's probably why they call it husbandry. He's better at it than the last one — bodes well for the marriage, don't you think?

He's also already started a dozen different species of plants in little trays I keep tripping over in the hall. He's planted a whole bunch of herbs, 'cause we both like fresh oregano and basil and other herb-like substances in our food.

He's also started tomatoes, jalapenos, onions, and various other things I wouldn't eat on a bet, but it makes him happy.

I, on the other hand remember the jalapeno plants late last summer that were buried in hailstones up to what would have been their elbows if they had elbows.

Don't want to crush his dreams or anything, but I hate the thought of putting a lot of effort into greenery that will get beaten to death in the summer hailstorms.

Trying to be optimistic about the whole thing, but when I look outside this morning, it looks cold and crunchy. The tumbleweeds are rolling in the winds that won't slow down, and the urban tumbleweeds composed of plastic bags are stuck to every fence line in town.

I know spring will surely come, but in the meantime, I'm thinking out loud my husband's been a wee bit optimistic in terms of when it's actually going to show up.

I also know that Yankee groundhog predicted we were going to have six more weeks of winter, but then again, what would a northern rodent know about West Texas weather anyway?

I think I'll go make myself a cup of hot cocoa and dream of spring greenery.

I lift my eyes up to the hills of West Texas

Looking out the sliding glass doors at a backyard frosted in the cool, early spring moonlight, every surface is gilded by white gold in sharp relief, a moment of stark beauty before the desert awakens. A gray-black cat, searching for a mouse to snack on, scuds across the yard like a fallen leaf blowing in the Fort Stockton wind.

Branches on the trees that winter has stripped of leaves gently dance against the ghostly glow of a pre-dawn, moonlit sky, reaching up with thousands of slender fingers toward the cloud that dims the landscape for just a moment, and is gone.

Driving down quiet back streets, the windows of every silent, stilled car and truck are covered by the condensation from heavy dew. Each seems to stare inwards at something only they can see, contemplating some mechanical infinity far beyond their makers' intent.

The land continues to brighten as the sun lightens the plateaus to the east, bathing everything in a rosy glow that softens the edges of the buildings and fence lines. More vehicles are moving now, trucks rumbling by, cars taking children to school, adults to work, school bus reflectors impossibly bright.

People don't ruin this landscape—we are part of it, all of us. This, finally, is where the tree-hugging environmentalists and I part ways. They see humans as a cancer on this land, a contaminant, something that needs to be cured. It is the ultimate in self-hatred.

You've heard "beauty is in the eye of the beholder," right? In my opinion, without a beholder, there is no beauty. The rabbit doesn't sit looking across the acre she can see and think "Ah, there's beauty in that cactus I'm about to run towards." Her miniscule capacity for thought is wound around her instincts. Survival for herself and her kits is pretty much her complete focus.

Once our basic needs are met, humans, on the other hand, are capable of recognizing and appreciating beauty, whether from nature or built by mankind. Have you walked in the county courthouse lately? Gorgeous, imposing inside and out.

Have you ever really looked at the cloverleaf overpasses in the big cities? Their soaring beauty is ignored, dismissed, disrespected, but some engineer had to be able to think conceptually in a very large and imposing way, and then men and women made that concept a reality.

Fort Stockton, too, has its own occasional splendor. I love the Spanish-style houses, stucco with bright red tile roofs. Spanish homes have been built in that fashion for centuries, light-colored to reflect the heat wherever possible, around a courtyard to protect the inhabitants, built to take advantage of every slightest breeze to cool the interior.

The fruit trees are beginning to bloom, and much like the humans who live here, those are transplanted from other surroundings, other climates. Their beauty is softer, sweeter than the in-your-face presence of the native plants, the spiky reality of a prickly pear, the tumbleweed seemingly made of razor-wire.

Life gets so busy we forget to even look... but I try very, very hard to look around me, to try to see what's there, to notice the sunrise, and the sunset.

The clocks change soon, and I'll be getting to work in the dark again very soon, so I'm enjoying every moment I can.

The day's work done, I head home once more through the hustle and bustle of Fort Stockton. After dinner, tired, replete, I sit on the tiny little patch of concrete that is the precursor to a patio yet to come.

The gorgeous sunset lights up the west in red and gold, turning the plateaus into shadowless purple silhouettes. It always reminds of one of the Psalms, "I will lift up mine eyes unto the hills…"

I look out over the fruit trees we planted this past weekend, peaches, plums, pomegranates, cherries. My ever-optimistic, Alaskan-born husband could not grow these up there, and wants to see if he can grow them here.

I'm thinking out loud, if these tiny little sticks we planted so hopefully grow and survive the heat and the hailstorms, this time next year, my back yard will be truly beautiful. I'll be looking for it.

Opinions are a good thing, I hear everybody has 'em

Opinion is defined as: "the expression of a belief that is held with confidence." I've got lots of opinions. For instance, I believe spring is the best season of the year in Fort Stockton. Now that's an opinion, and it's based on the evidence of the last two years spent here.

Y'all might have different opinions, but this one's mine.

It's also my opinion that, when the good Lord was handing out smarts, he skipped a few people.

I've been witness to more stupidity this last week than is usually my misfortune... it was apparently Gomer's big day out. Like the guy riding one of those zippy little foreign motorcycles on the interstate this week.

The big goober was drafting behind vehicles, riding within ten feet or even closer to the rear bumper of everything from SUVs to eighteen-wheel trucks. If there had been just one piece of road trash they centered their tires over, he would have been dead as a doorknob. We finally had to speed up and quit watching him.

On the brighter side, we drove by the silhouette of the cavalry soldiers a little east of

Fort Stockton, and that looks pretty darned awesome. Now that's also an opinion. Some people will like it, some people won't, but I like it.

I also believe there are a fair few people who continue to push Fort Stockton toward a brighter decade to come. Stop Doug May on the street sometime and get him talking about what the next economic coup is he's orchestrated. He's always got something up his sleeve and is never boring.

I know it can get annoying to listen to folks who are relentlessly positive. And my every opinion about Fort Stockton isn't completely positive, I swear.

I still think we need more street signs in a number of places. We also need stop signs in more than a few places.

Then again, we also need to teach a whole bunch of people what "Stop" actually means. That is also an opinion.

Many of our vacant lots also look blinking awful in the bright spring sunshine, both overgrown and trashed out. Did you know there's a city ordinance saying your grass can't be more than a foot tall? I didn't either until last week.

Another of those not-so-Miss-Mary-Sunshine opinions is my abiding dislike of insurance companies. I know some lovely people who are insurance agents, and this is not about them. It's the whole concept of insurance.

Here's what it boils down to: It is not to the company's benefit to pay your claim. Period. Whether it's life, health, home, vehicle or any other insurance, the reasoning is exactly the same. Their bottom line is affected badly if they carry through on the promises they've made.

This is not a good business model for those who are forced to need their services.

So, they hedge all promises in the small print, and the ones who end up paying the tab are folks like you and me.

So there's my litany of just a few of my many opinions.

It is now time for me to speculate on what's for breakfast.

Don't have an opinion yet, but I'm thinking out loud I'm leaning toward a toasted English muffin.

How about you?

Water, water everywhere; it's time to stop and think!

I've been watching all the flap about Texas House Bill 4805 going past, with rhetoric a-plenty in both directions. I swear I did my best to read the text of that bill.

I consider myself, wrongly or rightly, to be a little smarter than your average bear, and that was still just incomprehensible.

It did appear anyone within 130 miles of Midland/Odessa would be affected. And the only number I could get my head around is the one those who oppose the bill keep throwing around. Bill 4805 would allow Midland/Odessa to pump 41 million gallons of water a day out of the aquifers that supply our county.

So, because I'm math-challenged, I stuck that figure into a computer to see what I could figure out.

Here are some of the equivalencies. If you make $9.85 an hour, the distinguished gentleman pushing this bill in the local area will make approximately your year's salary every single day. And that's if he's profiting only one half of one tenth of a penny for each gallon that heads toward our neighbors to the northwest.

Over the course of a year, he stands to pull in $7.4 million dollars at that price.

What am I basing that price on? Not a dern thing. I have no idea if this is how much profit would accrue for this. I've tried to believe that, if I was going to make a $20,000 a day from it, I would have enough scruples not to stick a big giant straw down in the water table and start siphoning it off into our neighbors water towers.

I don't think I would do that. But dang, that's a lot of money.

I just hope I would have sense enough not to destroy the lives and livelihoods of one set of people to benefit another.

Speaking of sense, the other thing that bothers me about this is that, after only a year of living here, I know when irrigation begins, surface water dries up. And I also know this has been brought up to that same gentleman more than once, at varying levels of volume.

Look, I grew up in Texas, and am not a tree-hugger. That would be a tough job description in West Texas anyway. Have you ever hugged a mesquite tree?

Perforation is no fun.

However, sucking that much water out of the aquifers on a daily basis is going to turn this county into a dust bowl. And it is already dusty around here.

Every time I think about it, I just have this vision of a Pecos County sinkhole opening up, about a hundred feet deep, and the entire county dropping into it with a "whoomp!" sound.

It's hard enough to get me to drive up to Odessa now to go to the Super Walmart. If I have to climb a ladder to do it, I'm never going to leave.

If you're upset enough about this, you Pecos County residents need to call your state representatives and tell them how you feel about it. You don't have to tell them about the sinkhole thing, but the rest of this might serve to get your conversation started. Feel free to plagiarize.

The above opinions are mine and mine alone, not necessarily those of the management, and I'm just thinking out loud.

Swear.

Please don't shoot me before my second cup of coffee

This Monday morning finds me scrambling around in that day-after-vacation's-over, where-the-heck-did-I-put-my-socks, fuzzy sort of operation.

I still have to make the husband's lunch, take my own shower, wake up the boy to take his shower, find everything I need to have at work, and all the other habitual things that usually flow along pretty well most Monday mornings.

Oh, and get this piece done, can't forget that.

This morning it feels like somebody poured brake fluid in my transmission. Sort of slipping and revving, and moving forward with a jerk, then slipping again. On my second cup of coffee, and it's just beginning to clear away the fog.

We loved being away for a week, especially staying with family we missed and were glad to see, but really loved coming back. There's nothing like being with your own stuff when you haven't seen it for a while.

Really felt at home last night about 8:30, when I stepped into our backyard and looked up into a clear sky full of stars.

We stayed the week in Kingsville, down south past Corpus Christi.

Kingsville's got about 25,000 people, and there was just way too much light for the stars to be seen. I love looking up and seeing Orion striding across the sky. It happens to be the only constellation besides the Big Dipper I actually recognize, but it's enough.

Heard there was snow again while we were gone. Wasn't sorry we missed that. Kinda done with snow and cold temperatures this year; had enough of winter in general, want to see a little springtime before the summertime gets here and elbows it aside in a heated exchange.

One thing I always do when traveling is compare Fort Stockton to other towns that range in size from much smaller than us, like Sanderson, and much larger, such as Kingsville, and all the sizes in between.

There is a Texas-type Main Street that seems to be pretty much the norm, and while parts of our downtown are an exception, there are similarities. The number of vacant buildings increases as you move north of the post office and south of the courthouse, with a little core of thriving businesses.

Ever been to Uvalde? Stayed the night there Saturday night. Uvalde's downtown is basically antique hunter's heaven. Few vacant buildings, lots of activity. Nice town, though it's pretty darned obvious that deer hunting is the main industry outside of farming.

Even the grocery store had deer blinds for sale, or whatever you call those boxes on stilts hunters hide in to lay in wait for the deer.

Oh, and this is seriously just my opinion, but I believe putting out deer corn and basically teaching deer here is a safe place to eat with plenty of food is cheating.

Hardly seems fair to position the hunter within rifle shot of the deer feeder and then pick 'em off when they come to get breakfast some morning.

It would be like standing outside my kitchen window and shooting me when I go to get my coffee. Too easy! That's not hunting, it's target practice. You know I can't survive without it.

Admittedly, to this point, I've never been shot at while standing in front of the coffeemaker, so I'm conditioned to believe it's safe. Well, up to now, anyway.

Anyway, to drag it back to the subject, Stockton's somewhere in the middle in terms of our downtown vitality — part of the problem, of course, that the interstate is a fair chunk away from downtown. Not sure how to fix that, but I'm sure somebody's got an idea about it.

Well, I'm running out of time just as I ran out of words. I'm thinking out loud I'm going to go close my kitchen curtains and get this Monday rolling.

Here's hoping nobody's taking potshots when I go get that last cup of coffee...

Just wondering…
Why do we live here again?

After my article tweaking a certain gentleman for his plan to ship the water underlying Pecos County to supply nice green lawns for the folks in Midland/Odessa, I started thinking about why exactly people have lived in and around Fort Stockton for 150 years.

Opinions vary, but a large part may be because it lies at a crossroads between larger communities.

To get from San Antonio to El Paso, you just about have to come through the region. Austin to El Paso, same thing.

If you're heading from the Big Bend region into Midland/Odessa, Abilene, Lubbock, Amarillo, you pretty much also come through Fort Stockton.

Comanche Springs was also the third biggest fresh water source in all of Texas in the mid-19th century, which makes it a sensible decision on the part of the Army to build the fort here in 1859.

If you look at maps of the United States, most cities are based around water of some kind. Large cities are almost always based either next to or very near some form of viable fresh water source.

The Butterfield Overland Stage Route also went through here, and the area was a favorite stopping place for those headed for the state of Chihuahua, in Mexico. Still doesn't explain why people stay and have stayed for a century and a half.

Went looking on the Internet for research on why people live in communities at all, and the answer basically boiled down to "we're not sure."

The stuff written by the ones that were willing to jump off the fence one way or another was either insufferably tree-hugger-mugger or new-age-ish, or boiled down to survival of the fittest.

In other words, they believe the ones that went out in the desert and died because they didn't have enough water had a tendency to not have descendants.

The folks still in Fort Stockton are probably descended from the ones that had sense enough to set up camp near water and develop food sources. And, when people cooperate, they're more likely to survive.

It's sort of a simplistic answer, and I tend to be a simple person, so I'm willing to accept that as the premise for how it started. I can easily envision one cowboy saying to another, "You watch my back and I'll watch yours," in a very umm, no, this-is-not-Brokeback-Mountain kind of way.

The Comanche tribe for which Comanche Springs is named were still a little touchy about that time, with their country being yanked out from under them and all. So military occupation of Fort Stockton began around 1859 to keep travelers safe before the Unpleasantries Between the States.

It was re-established in 1867 after the aforementioned war was done and all over but the carpetbagging.

The second wave was mainly composed of the Buffalo Soldiers, the black soldiers that were such a key part of keeping the West safe for travelers.

Not sure where the Buffalo Soldiers went, but I'm pretty sure very few of them are living here now. Don't know why they didn't stay.

There are a lot of questions I can't answer about why everyone reading this lives here, but I can tell you how I ended up here. Two reasons — family first, and then money. When I headed for Texas some while ago, I had two choices. I could head for Nacogdoches in Deep East Texas to stay with my brother, or Fort Stockton in West Texas to stay with my sister until I got on my feet.

So, because I'm a big geeky girl, I checked both cities out on one of the coolest web sites I know.

It's www.city-data.com, and you can find out just about anything you want to know about a specific city there. One statistic in particular kind of shocked me.

In Nacogdoches, in 2007, the unemployment rate for people of my gender was 9.9 percent. In Fort Stockton, that rate was 3.6 percent for women. Basically, if a woman wants to work here, she can work.

I'm thinking out loud that after all that, I know why I'm here, but the question remains: Why are you here?

It's a dry heat you know...
kinda like an oven

Sometimes we humans end up with bad outcomes, no matter what our intentions may be. It is fairly typical of human endeavor overall—we do nothing by halves. Full-out, fastest, highest, longest, tallest, deepest, best, we want them all.

Speaking of which, have you checked out the Chamber of Commerce at Dickinson and Main Street? And yes, I know you know where it is if you live here, but we do get the occasional visitor in Fort Stockton, you know.

The stone work is awesome, and I can't wait to see the water feature when it's fully operational, and the silhouettes are just outstanding. I hope they're prepared to have people climbing all over that stuff to take pictures.

I'm fully expecting to see someone riding on the back of Paisano Pete, the giant roadrunner, one of these days, with their mom snapping pictures below.

For the uninitiated, Paisano Pete stands at the corner of the main drag of Fort Stockton, Dickinson Street and Main Street. Erected in 1980, and renovated in 2014, he was declared a True Texas Icon as Town Mascot in the

September 2011 issue of Texas Highways magazine. The townsfolk dress him up for Easter and Christmas.

I have no big point to make with this piece – I'm typing like mad at 6:15 on a Monday morning, and trying to dry the sweat off of my hands so I don't short out the keyboard or my mouse. Just got off the elliptical machine, and I'm a little glowy, if you prefer that for the female of the species. I genuinely don't mind sweating as long as it's my idea.

And it was not my idea to get that sweaty last week. The thermometer under my carport showed 113 degrees on Saturday. And my sister, whom I love dearly, decided on Friday she wanted to have the yard sale she's been preparing for over the last six weeks or so. And she wanted to hold it on Saturday. I said a few choice words, but it's family, you know, so I went over to help out.

During the course of the day on Saturday, I drank three big ol' Route 44 size unsweet teas from Sonic and still lost five pounds running around out there. Seriously. We started hauling stuff out to her yard at 4 a.m., put the signs out at 6 a.m., and then stayed out there until about 2 p.m. She was still getting rid of stuff about 9 on Saturday night.

And, of course, I forgot two of the signs when I went to take them down, so she had people showing up in her yard even after we shut it all down—said she made another $15 that way.

I've done worse things, and been in worse heat. Many years ago, I moved to Las Vegas with the now-ex-husband, to his last Air Force assignment at Nellis Air Force Base. We got there in early August, and it was 129 degrees the day we arrived. I thought I had gone to hell, literally.

But, you learn to survive, and you just go outside at night—another reason Las Vegas is up all night. It's too dang hot to go outside during the day. I drove to the store one afternoon, stuck my car keys in my pocket when I walked inside. Burned myself from the key retaining the heat from the steering column.

Everyone says it's a dry heat—but I'm thinking out loud an oven is dry heat, too. I went home to see my mama in East Texas for a week while we were stationed there in Vegas, and I remember just standing out in the rain. She thought I was crazy.

I'm thinking out loud she might have been right.

Garage sales: Texas state sport

There are some really terrific things about living here, and some not-so-spiffy things.

Spiffy: Love the fact yard sales and garage sales are practically a town sport. Not a weekend goes by, no matter how hot or cold, there isn't at least one.

Not-So-Spiffy: Street signs! Where the heck are the street signs in so many parts of town? For those of us who haven't lived here all our lives, it's terribly frustrating to find the sales that are on unmarked streets.

Also not so spiffy is the rude behavior at many of the sales. If you really want that 10-cent plaque with the picture of the sheep saying "Ewe aint' fat, ewe's fluffy!," just ask for it, don't snatch it out of my hand.

If you wouldn't do it to your mama, don't do it to me.

Spiffy: The public library is absolutely outstanding, including a bank of Internet-connected computers, bilingual book selections and a top-notch interlibrary loan program.

They bring in musicians and performers regularly in the evenings, have a great writer's workshop, as well as a crochet and other workshops in the evenings. Just ask 'em. There's something always going on. The folks that work there are always kind, chatty and a tremendous resource. I've seen smaller, dimmer, dingier libraries in towns twice and three times this size.

Not-So-Spiffy: That little kid who coughs on the keyboards on the computers. Ew.

Spiffy: The number and strength of community services agencies and volunteers. Apparently, this town is most responsive to specific volunteer requests. When asked, people stand up and get the job done over and over again.

Not-So-Spiffy: That so many folks need help. That, unfortunately, seems to be universal.

Spiffy: This country. I love this country, from the mesquites to the wildflowers to everything in between. Deer, elk, javelin, foxes, roadrunners, quail, you name it, it's here. People who think the desert is a bare, sandy, lifeless land just haven't been here.

Not-So-Spiffy: Those big red signs that say S-T-O-P? They do not mean "roll through," or "hit your brakes and keep going," and they absolutely do not mean "yield," as in look and go anyway. They mean stop, dang it! So STOP.

Ahem. Sorry about that last little rant there. I'm just thinking out loud.

Can love of a place conquer the love of money?

Love is when the welfare of another is more important than your own. In my opinion, we are remembered for and defined by who and what we love, not how much money we make.

I'll get back to that idea before I'm done, but just in case you haven't been reading the paper, the neighbor's once again pushing to sell the water out from under Pecos County, to the tune of 49,000 acre feet per year. I had to look up what "acre-foot" means.

Sensibly enough, it's the amount of water it takes to cover an acre of land to the depth of one foot, or 325,981 gallons. This means he wants to sell more than 14 billion gallons a year out of the aquifers we depend on. You read that correctly, that's 14 billion, with a "b."

According to the same article from last week, when Comanche Springs began flowing again in February of last year, it was flowing at a rate of eight million gallons a day, averaging out to about three billion gallons a year.

I know I'm dang ignorant about hydrogeology, so correct me if I'm wrong, but if there is "extra" water in the aquifers, it must go somewhere, and this is how an aboveground spring is formed. On the face of it, it appears if the neighbor's scheme goes through, it will most likely dry up Comanche Springs and still siphon another 35 million gallons from the local aquifers each and every day. Yep, I said 35 million gallons a day.

The gentleman commissioned a study to see if this is feasible, and lo and behold, that study shows you could take up to 26 billion gallons a year and not affect other users of the water. Those "other users," by the way, are us. You and me and the rest of us who like to shower in the morning, water the plants once a month or so before they're dead, put out fires, and so on.

I have done a fair amount of research in my life, and a study commissioned by the person who stands to benefit from the results is not exactly seen as unbiased.

I'm sure the folks that did that study are perfectly nice, and fully believe their results are correct. However, it's an unfortunate facet of human nature--if a study says what the person or organization who commissioned it wants it to say, it's seen as biased. If it says what the payer doesn't want it to say, it's seen as unbiased.

In other words, if McDonald's funded a study, and the results showed Big Macs cure cancer, we would be just a teensy bit suspicious, yes? Study or no study, it's tough to believe that sucking that much water out of the aquifers is not going to affect the rest of us "users" in any way.

I don't know if this can be stopped. As far as I know, if he wants to sell the water out from under his own land, there's nothing we can do but watch.

To yank this back around to the beginning, I have been trying of late to teach my 15-year-old the definition of love in the first paragraph of this article. It's hard for a teen-aged boy to look beyond his own immediate wants to what other people need, and I know that, so I'm trying to be patient.

I would think that our neighbor, however, was old enough to know better. Now, to give him the benefit of the doubt, he may be doing this 'cause he needs to pay off his electric bill. This tough economy has hit everybody, even the rich folks. But I can tell you this much: if our neighbor loves West Texas, if he loves Pecos County, if he gives one teeny-tiny rat's patootie about Fort Stockton, he will not sell the water out from under us to make a buck. Or millions of bucks, for that matter.

Do you love your family? Your home? Your community? Then it's time to speak up. If you love this place, if you care about life as we know it in Fort Stockton, then start talking to the Water Board, to your City Councilmember, to your Congress-critters, both state and federal, and to the aforementioned neighbor, if you happen to know him.

If you love your children, and would like them to have enough water to survive in this desert we call home, you might want to make yourself heard about right now.

You don't have to take this seriously, you know, I'm just thinking out loud. But you might want to if you plan to raise your kids here.

This amazing country astonishes, still

I'm sitting tapping away on my laptop at the Fort Stockton Public Library on a Saturday afternoon, as we've been without power out at the ranch since Thursday morning about 3 a.m.

Didn't want to miss my Monday deadline, but don't know if we'll actually have power out at the ranch by Monday, and don't want to drive 45 minutes just to hit "send" on an e-mail.

Kinda funny that way.

The eastern side of the ranch looked, this morning, like it had been candied with clear sugar syrup. It was dripping at every edge, and with the merest breath of wind, an entire tree would shrug off its coating of ice all at once, with a resounding crash.

We drove all the way across the ranch, and came out on Highway 385, just to check and see if anyone else had stuck out the storm. We didn't see anyone, but they may, like us, have taken the first opportunity to get into town and get a few supplies to finish out the weekend.

The west side of the ranch just looked a little damp, as if there had never been a storm... but the howling wind explained the quick thaw on that side.

It's a little strange to live someplace where you and your nearest neighbor can be experiencing two completely different weather patterns.

Had to hook up the generator for a little while last night just to find out what the weather was like around the area, and got a complete shock seeing how much it snowed in Midland and Odessa.

We thought we had it bad with the electricity out, but at least we're not trying to deal with snow on top of it. We did hear the roads were icy throughout the area, which is why we waited until this morning to come into town.

Saw more than a few places where we could tell from the highway that the electric lines were down. My friend asked me if I called them in—I told her I didn't have enough life left to stay on hold that long.

I can't imagine what it would be like working for the electric company this weekend, or for the week to come, for that matter. For this week, though, guys, with every line you hook up, you are going to be heroes to somebody.

We're luckier than some—we have a fireplace, including a gas starter line to it, which probably saw more use in the last two days than it has in the last two years. We also have a gas stove that works as long as you light it and don't wait for an electric starter that isn't going to work.

And we have hot water, thanks to a gas water heater, and a gravity-feed water tank that has, so far, lasted. We're hoping the electricity comes back on that pumps water up to the water tank before we have to start hauling water.

What we don't have is the phone or the Internet. It's been oddly pleasant, disconnecting. I figured the kids would be just frantic, as we've been out of touch almost 48 hours, but come to find out, if they were worried, they weren't telling anybody. Neither was my boss, who didn't e-mail me or anything. If they tried to phone, of course, we just don't know.

Haven't decided whether to be upset because no one missed us, or relieved.

It's a pretty serene life, once you stop flicking the light switches without thinking. It also gives you a lot of insight into what you need most and what you don't need.

We need books to read and light to read them by.

We apparently don't need TV unless we really want to know what's happening in the outside world, because we've watched it very little, even when we do have the generator going.

We need water. If I don't get a shower on a regular and ongoing basis, I get to be Miss Crankypants.

My husband apparently needs coffee. As testimony, the fact that he was beating coffee beans in a plastic bag the last couple of mornings, using the bottom of a pan. And then a rolling pin. It worked. Which meant I didn't have to live with Mister Crankypants.

I appreciated that.

And, I appreciated the sight of a prickly pear with every single needle coated in ice.

I'm thinking out loud I could have actually reached out and touched one without picking stickers out of my finger for days.

Still didn't risk it.

Epitaphs

I left epitaphs for last because they are, by their nature, sad, and this is not, overall, a sad book.

Some are epitaphs for careers, some for people I have loved from a distance, like Leonard Nimoy, and the last two are for my mother, who I grieve for still. I wrote them many years apart. Grief is a jouney.

Just warning you there may be a smile here and there, but these are truly from sad and serious places in my heart.

Lisa C Hannon

Epitaph for a career

At one time or another, I may have said I was five feet two inches tall. I must confess, I am not. On my really good days, I'm five foot one and three-quarter inches tall. On my bad days, I'm five foot one. And, when I hang my head in shame because I fibbed, I'm pretty close to being a "little person" in terms of height.

There, I said it. I've bared my soul in public; I've acknowledged I lied.

Brian Williams, the news anchor for CBS, is no longer in the news. He is yesterday's news now, a footnote to entertainment history, at best. He was suspended and probably quietly fired by now for fibbing about riding in a helicopter that was hit by a rocket-propelled grenade.

Unlike Williams, I will not be suspended, lambasted, excoriated and in general made to feel like I'm an ax murderer for fibbing. And, unlike him, I will also be allowed to continue writing for the public.

So, what's the difference?

First, of course, is scale.

Williams, bless his heart, fibbed in front of umpty-million people. I am willing to predict with some certainty that the number of folks who read this essay will be fewer than the number of viewers for his "conflation" of his experience.

Another part of the difference is his assumption, whether conscious or not, that no one was going to call him on it. I know someone's going to call me on my fib. My husband gives me the horse laugh every time I claim to be five feet two. Accompanied by a snort of derision.

Williams' audience included the people who knew the truth, too, but they weren't snorting. He said at one point during the news breaking around him he "wasn't trying to steal anyone's valor."

That's probably true. He was simply trying to portray someone brave, strong, tough and heroic. Riding in a chopper in a war zone just wasn't enough to make him feel brave, I guess.

The phrase "war story" is a part of the American lexicon.

When I was in the U.S. Air Force, it was used by veterans and active-duty military alike as slang to denote the vaguely fictional, always hilarious stories swapped by comrades in arms about their experiences in their fields of operation.

Please note—we didn't question the stories—they were supposed to be at least slightly fuzzy around the edges. You played down the scary parts unless you could make them funny.

Full disclosure: While I am a vet, I was never under fire. I spent an awful lot of time with people who were, especially in the missile fields in Montana.

I do have a few war stories, though. Most of them involve those missile fields. For instance, I was delivering a dinner tray to the missile officer in the command center in one of those ICBM launch facilities, circa 1982.

When the blast door opened, a very large officer stood there in footie pajamas, gun belted around his hip. I'm sure I was grinning, because he glared and said, "My feet were cold!" Snatching the tray out of my hands, he couldn't get that door closed fast enough.

Is it true? Did I "conflate" it from other people's experiences? I don't think so, but I wouldn't testify to it. So I'll probably continue to tell that story to friends at dinner parties.

OK, that's actually a lie. Oh, not the friends part—I have friends. But I try really hard not to ever go to dinner parties.

And that's where I have a hard time understanding all this. Williams' job put him in the glare of the public eye nearly every day. Why would one of the foremost news anchors in the country feel driven to seek more attention so badly he was willing to leave the truth behind?

Now, personally, I think it's been a long time since broadcast news was the whole truth and nothing but. But, this is not about what he said on his newscasts. It all began with what he said in conversation with David Letterman while trying not just to maintain, but inflate his celebrity status.

It's about what happens when news people become the news. And about idols with feet of clay, who want to be celebrities more than they want to tell the truth.

Americans find it hard to feel sorry for someone making $10 million a year who got caught lying.

But I do.

Why? Because I'm rattling away on a keyboard, trying to find something even remotely funny in a situation where a man's integrity and honesty throughout his entire career ended up being scrutinized word by word. And he lost his job, and he lost everything. And it's not funny. It's sad.

He got that extra dollop of fame he wanted.

But I'm thinking out loud I'd just as soon be five feet, one and three-quarter inches tall.

And not famous.

Love and loss knows no logic

I have something to confess. I tend to avoid knowing much about the people behind television characters I dearly love.

Best examples would include Sheldon Cooper in "The Big Bang Theory," Heathcliff Huxtable of "The Cosby Show" and Spock from "Star Trek."

The women who have accused Bill Cosby of some form of rape are, unfortunately, a case in point. These women who spoke up about something that has tortured them for years have completely destroyed Cosby's legacy without his ever being able to refute those charges in the justice system.

He has been tried, found guilty and sentenced to the margins of our society in the court of public opinion. I can't help but believe them, from sheer numbers alone.

It is past horrifying for them. And the rest of us will never be able to watch "The Cosby Show" or any of his comedy routines or read any of his books without wondering.

We loved all those things—but they're beyond redemption. I just can't unsee the images these women have drawn. And most of them hope for nothing more than finally speaking of their trauma. The statute of limitations is long past. Justice isn't always swift.

On another note, without nearly as much trauma, I accidentally clicked on a YouTube video of Jim Parsons, the man who plays Sheldon Cooper, talking about how he quit smoking.

It wasn't the fact he smoked that bothered me—I'm an ex-smoker, as well. It was that he laughed. Sheldon Cooper shouldn't laugh. Jim Parsons (of course) does. I don't know why it bothered me. It just did. I want Parsons to remain Sheldon Cooper forever. It's a vain hope, but I never said my reluctance to acknowledge reality was rational.

The other addition to my weird, rule-based system was Leonard Nimoy and his indelibly iconic characterization of Spock in "Star Trek" and all its follow-on movies. "Star Trek's" initial run was between my sixth and ninth years, and I have zero memory of ever seeing it at that time.

Well, it wouldn't have been my dad's kind of thing. And, since my father was the monarch of the remote control, it was a foregone conclusion I wouldn't see it. Of course I was the remote control, as in "Go change the dial to Channel 4. OK, try Channel 6. No, I won't watch that crap, go back to Channel 3."

Throughout the latter 1960s, I mostly remember "The Lawrence Welk Show" and "Bonanza," the mention of which makes me hum the theme music every time. Have you seen the picture of Dan Blocker (who played Hoss in "Bonanza") in the mural in Alpine? I didn't know he went to Sul Ross State University until we explored our neighbor to the south. But I digress.

Once "Star Trek" ootched its way by the skin of its teeth into syndication, one of the three TV stations we received began showing it every afternoon.

School days, after we got off the bus, my sis and I were glued to the TV. "Dialing for Dollars Theatre" was still on when we turned the TV on, and at 4 p.m., "Star Trek" would come on.

I watched every episode. And then watched them all again, because I had a massive crush on Spock.

All my friends loved Captain Kirk. Not me. I had a thing for the pointy-eared logician who forever struggled with his too-human half. Spock will apparently always be part of my heart.

When they killed him off in the one movie, I cried as if my heart would break, something my then-husband found quite baffling.

Like Jim Parsons, it was always a jolt to see Nimoy smile. Which makes me wonder why I have a thing for characters who have trouble expressing emotions. Oddly enough, so did my ex-husband. Huh.

Of course, I tend to live with all my emotions up front, out in everybody's face—so perhaps it's their control I would like to emulate.

Nimoy passed away from the effects of chronic obstructive pulmonary disease, even though he had given up smoking 30 years prior to his death. It seems a hard way to die, and I hope he was not in pain or distress toward the end.

But I'm thinking out loud Leonard Nimoy indeed lived long and prospered. In the end, he created an identity for his life and his legacy that was respected as much as the character we all loved so much.

It's a fitting epitaph, one anyone can respect. And perhaps someday, I'll even be able to see a picture of him smiling without flinching.

Losing Mama,
seven months after

You know, it's funny how casually we use phrases with "died" or "killed," and we really don't realize it most of the time: "I could have just died when she said that," or "I could have killed him when he did that," or various other innocuous, didn't-mean-it-like-that phrases.

I've been thinking about that a lot lately. For a lot of reasons.

As I write this, a few more days will mean Mama will be gone seven months now. I miss her. I'm beginning to think I always will.

The facts and dates of Mama's life are interesting only to those of us who loved her, but a quick snapshot might help. She was born Vivian Marie, in Center, Texas, in 1926. Married four times, she bore seven children and died July 16, 1999.

Those 22 words are sparse indeed to describe someone surrounded by her children and grandchildren as she died. All begged her to wake up, to come back, to take one more breath. She was loved as few people are in this life, unreservedly, unconditionally, by a family that was shattered by her death.

In the two weeks before she died, all six of her surviving children spoke to her at length or traveled to see her. I went up to Cushing, Texas, where she lived, for coffee. My sisters spoke to her at length on the phone, one from North Texas, one from Maine.

My brother came down from Nebraska with his wife and grandson, another brother traveled the 20 miles from Nacogdoches, Texas, with his daughter. And the other brother who lived right next door had stuck his head in to say goodbye before he left for his job on an offshore drilling rig.

I had a chance, the day I went up for coffee, to sit in my favorite spot, on the floor, next to her chair, while we watched TV. I still feel her fingers stroking my hair in my dreams.

Every moment with my mother was treasured; I think we all knew we weren't going to have her for long. She seemed healthy, but we knew how much damage the seven heart attacks had caused over the 20 years prior. Every time I hugged her, she seemed a little more fragile, the bones nearer the skin.

My mother was why I was at Texas A&M working on my master's degree, and why we lived in Madisonville, halfway between the university and her house.

It was the first time since I married my Air Force husband I was able to say—"I want to go home to Texas," and actually make it happen.

After 20 years of living in other states, other countries, thousands of miles away from her, I had barely a year where I could see her most weekends.

It wasn't enough.

When I got there, her eyes were tightly closed, but she still said a few words occasionally. She put her hands out in front of her, moving them apart as if opening a curtain, and murmured, "That's it! It's a tunnel!" They were the last words she ever spoke.

The doctors tried to stop the bleeding into her brain without success. Hours of agonized waiting and floods of tears led to the bedside watch. Her poor, battered heart took four hours to finally stop beating, but she never took another breath.

I can't make you or anyone understand what she was to me, to all of us. But if you've ever lost someone that close, you know. The circumstances change, but the love remains the same.

She would be so upset with me for grieving like this. But she is on my mind today, every day.

And every moment that I'm just thinking out loud.

There is no loss worse than the one you loved first... but time wears off the jagged edges

I recently went on my semi-regular pilgrimage to visit the cemetery where my mother was buried ten years ago.

Mama, among many other things, was proof you can grow up to be a decent human being as long as you have one good parent. She lived both sides of that equation. She was barely two years old when her father ran off, and she was my rock, as she was for the other six children she bore.

So, I went to where her headstone stands, and she wasn't there. That may sound a little odd — yes, she is buried there. But since she passed away, I have never felt her presence there.

When she died, I finished all the obligations I had that could be finished, and then, at 39 years old, I started running.

I left my master's degree program at Texas A&M and left my full-time job as a managing editor, and headed for Dallas. I guess I thought if I changed everything about the way I lived my life, some of the pain would stop.

A friend who had gone through a similar loss shook her head when I asked her, "When will I get over feeling this way?" Her answer was, "You don't, really. You just learn to live your life around the edges of that kind of grief."

After many, many years of being in the Air Force, and an Air Force wife stationed all over the world, I had the opportunity during the last year of her life to see my mother pretty much any time I wanted.

To say I was grateful for that sharply underestimates how much it meant to me. I will never forget sitting next to her chair while she watched TV—she took my hands in hers, and told me how beautiful my hands were. They weren't then and aren't now... but she had the eyes of the angels where her children were concerned.

A year and some months after Mama's death, I had for the umpteenth time driven home from work for 45 minutes through Dallas traffic, oblivious to everything, with tears running down my face. I could not seem to make things right, no matter how hard I tried.

Arriving home, I went in the bathroom to wash the tears away, and instead, I just lost it. I laid my head down on that bathroom counter, and I sobbed. When I lifted my head finally, and looked in the mirror, all I could see was a heartbroken girl who was committing that greatest of sins for a Southern woman. I simply couldn't cope.

I closed my eyes to shut away the sight, and for the first time since she had been gone, I felt my mother's arms around me... smelled her perfume... and heard her voice telling me she loved me, and she knew I'd do the right thing. When I opened my eyes, there was no one there.

That was the beginning of climbing out of that gaping hole she left behind when she went away. It was the beginning of realizing she left the way she would have wanted to, quickly, and without pain.

Climbing out of that grief began with some very successful decisions. I took some risks, but finally put my world into order pretty recently.

When you finally realize you will survive the greatest loss of your entire life, it makes you feel you can survive anything. Nothing the world could throw at me could be worse than losing her.

I'm sorry if this is a little scattered. I'm thinking out loud about this because a friend is burying his mother as I'm finishing up this article. I know he was able to be there during his mother's last moments. I know, too, the fact he was there will mean everything in the years to come.

She will be remembered, because she was loved.

She's Thinking Out Loud

Lisa C Hannon

About the Author

Lisa C Hannon's first novel, This Little Pig, A Flak Anders Mystery, is now available on Amazon.com in print and Kindle versions. Raised in the Deep East Texas setting of her novel, she is a veteran writer and editor of print, web and video content for business and industry, as well as newspaper articles, non-fiction and fiction.

She writes the Thinking Out Loud column for the weekly newspaper, The Fort Stockton Pioneer, and is an active member of the Critique Cafe' writers' workshop at the Fort Stockton Public Library, an hour's drive from the remote ranch where she and her husband now live in West Texas.

In her eclectic career, she's also worked as a librarian, a flight attendant, a fitness center manager and among other less savory occupations, an oilfield assistant controller, a consultant and a carnival ride operator.

Her awards include honors from the Texas Gulf Press Association for serious and humorous articles, and the national Telly Award for scriptwriting for a documentary on the U.S. Army.

She is blissfully married to Corey Hannon, who serves as a manager on the ranch where they live. They are extremely proud of their children, daughter Kelsey, who serves in the United States Army at Fort Leonard Wood, Missouri, and son John, who serves in the United States Air Force at Malmstrom Air Force Base, Montana. They also have two beautiful grandchildren.

Also by Lisa C Hannon

This Little Pig, a Flak Anders Mystery
Available on Amazon.com

Anita 'Flak' Anders, the first woman sheriff of Nacogdoches County, is called to a fire in the wee hours of a hot July night in Deep East Texas.

There she finds Curtis Lee Barnes, the husband who left her four years ago. He tells her the man trapped and dying in the burning building is the father-in-law he would never let her get to know.

While Flak struggles with her old flame, and the new relationship just beginning to develop with the fire chief, she must also figure out which of the Barnes family might have killed the old man. And Curtis Lee is among the suspects.

She better find out fast, as more bullets begin to fly, all apparently aimed at her head. While Flak dodges the escalating attempts on her life, the story of Tucker Barnes unfolds in alternating chapters.

The chilling evil of a man who abuses his family in every way is described by the youngest daughter, Jenny, who exposes the raw pain of a child and an adult searching for some way, any way, she could have made it different.

Against the backdrop of the religious fervor of the Pentecostal sects that proliferate in East Texas, Flak continues to pull the information she needs, piece by piece, out of a family that has banded together to shut out the outsider.

Piercing their defenses and gaining their trust, she finally puts all the pieces together just before her house explodes before her eyes. Concussed in the explosion, she has to take shelter with the fire chief she is beginning to love, and remember the solution to the puzzle before someone else dies.

She's Thinking Out Loud

www.ingramcontent.com/pod-product-compliance
Lightning Source LLC
La Vergne TN
LVHW051040080426
835508LV00019B/1624